Nibbana: Stream Winner to Arahantship

TEACHINGS OF THE BUDDHA

&

A GUIDE TO DEVELOPING THE VIEW OF A STREAM WINNER

By

DR ARIYATHUSHEL ARAHANT

Chennai • Bangalore

CLEVER FOX PUBLISHING
Chennai, India

Published by CLEVER FOX PUBLISHING 2024
Copyright © Dr Ariyathushel Arahant 2024

All Rights Reserved.
ISBN: 978-93-56488-60-1

This book has been published with all reasonable efforts taken to make the material error-free after the consent of the author. No part of this book shall be used, reproduced in any manner whatsoever without written permission from the author, except in the case of brief quotations embodied in critical articles and reviews.

The Author of this book is solely responsible and liable for its content including but not limited to the views, representations, descriptions, statements, information, opinions and references ["Content"]. The Content of this book shall not constitute or be construed or deemed to reflect the opinion or expression of the Publisher or Editor. Neither the Publisher nor Editor endorse or approve the Content of this book or guarantee the reliability, accuracy or completeness of the Content published herein and do not make any representations or warranties of any kind, express or implied, including but not limited to the implied warranties of merchantability, fitness for a particular purpose. The Publisher and Editor shall not be liable whatsoever for any errors, omissions, whether such errors or omissions result from negligence, accident, or any other cause or claims for loss or damages of any kind, including without limitation, indirect or consequential loss or damage arising out of use, inability to use, or about the reliability, accuracy or sufficiency of the information contained in this book.

Table of Contents

PREFACE 6

INTRODUCTION 7

Chapter One DHAMMA: STREAM ENTRY 10

Chapter Two NIBBANA: A BIRTH IN NOBLE LINAGE 35

Chapter Three BEYOND ORDINARY VIEWS: EGO, PRIDE, AND LIFESTYLE 38

Chapter Four TRAINING THE MIND 52

Chapter Five NIBBANA: THOUGHTS & SELF-VIEW 69

Chapter Six NIBBANA: TRAINING IN THOUGHTS & SAMSARA 73

Chapter Seven THE PRACTICE LEADING TO STREAM ENTRY 78

Chapter Eight CONFIDENCE IN TRIPLE GEM & STREAM ENTRY 84

Chapter Nine BEYOND ORDINARY VIEWS 90

Chapter Ten MIDDLE WAY 106

Chapter Eleven GRASPING & CLINGING 109

Chapter Twelve FETTERS 111

Chapter Thirteen VIPASSANA & NOBLE SEEING 116

Chapter Fourteen DHAMMA, NON-DHAMMA & DIFFERENT LEVELS OF PROGRESS 118

Chapter Fifteen USEFUL REFLECTIONS 122

Chapter Sixteen FURTHER THOUGHTS 133

*Namo Tassa Bhagavato Arahato
Sammā Sambuddhassa!*

Homage to the Blessed One, the Worthy One, the Supremely Enlightened One!

" Blessed One is fully accomplished, supremely enlightened, endowed with highest understanding and highest level of noble conduct, well-gone to Nibbana, the knower of worlds because he has known them in all ways, the
incomparable leader of men to be guided, the teacher of gods and humans, Buddha discovers the path to Nibbana: enlightened and showed us the way, distinguished by his special qualities: blessed one possess the highest of all beings."

Homage to the Blessed One!

PREFACE

In presenting this work, I record my immense loving kindness and genuine care towards the practitioners who are aspiring and practicing to gain Nibbana, and all.

I acknowledge contributions made by all Sangha towards preserving Dhamma.

INTRODUCTION

Cessation or Nibbana is the purpose and the key aspect of Buddha's teachings. Nibbana is gained through four stages. Nibbana leads to liberation from dissatisfaction and the four stages are a gradual process. Nibbana happens in its own time and is shaped by one's meritorious deeds and karmic influences.

Nibbana was sought and attained by many people during Buddha's time, and those who practice Dhamma in the right way will gain to a state of Stream Entry in their mind. To attain to a state of Stream Entry, one must gain an understanding of what Buddha has said and to train one's mind in line with Buddha's teachings.

What seems to be happening in the societies is that some of the common ways of understanding and practicing Dhamma have prevented Nibbana for those who understood and practiced in common ways. Some of the common ways of practicing Dhamma include practicing Dhamma as a meditation practice (such as living in the present moment), practicing Dhamma as a prerequisite to gaining an academic qualification, practicing Dhamma as a lifestyle, practicing Dhamma as learning or getting to know a language (for example, as Pali or Sanskrit), as reading books and remembering what is in books, and as exploring historical, cultural or philosophical aspects that were established related to the teaching of Buddha. Yet, these do not indicate the practice of Dhamma as Dhamma itself meaning "Sotapanna" leading to Nibbana across four stages.

Unlike in Buddha's time, when one could hear the teachings directly from Buddha or his enlightened disciples, in contemporary times, it is most common to hear about Dhamma as divisions or from ordinary disciples who are yet to develop a deep understanding of Dhamma for themselves. Ordinary views of Dhamma and various kinds of ordinary views, including divisions, are commonly heard and are available for people across societies and such views seem to have prevented Nibbana for practitioners for centuries, this is because to understand Nibbana, one needs to understand beyond common ways. Some of the common ways of practicing Dhamma include meditation practice or reading stories or discourses, including meditation practices to live in the present moment with an underlying tendency to identifying and clinging. A wise practitioner who has practiced Dhamma in common ways, such as by reading books and stories, exploring academic and historical aspects, and engaged in meditation and developing concentration for long without gaining a fruition might want to question the practitioner's own practice and reconsider practicing beyond ordinary ways. How to practice beyond ordinary ways depends on one's understanding and applying the understanding to one's daily life, a practice that requires full integration into one's daily life and lifestyle.

The teachings beyond ordinary views of Dhamma are rare, and those who wish to pursue the disciple route to reach a Stream Entry and gain benefit for themselves will need to reflect wisely and understand the teachings beyond ordinary views. Those who will hear and will practice Dhamma beyond common ways will gain a precious opportunity to enter the Stream-entry state, to develop higher knowledge, and to enter into Nibbana. Consequently, they will be able to stop experiencing stress and samsara for themselves.

The easiest way to develop vision leading to Nibbana is hearing Dhamma from someone who has already developed right understanding across four stages of Nibbana. Nibbana that is hard to see can be seen for those who develop internal qualities and wisdom to see Dhamma beyond ordinary views.

The purpose of this book is to clarify the teachings of Buddha leading to Nibbana beyond common views. Such clarification will be helpful for practitioners to develop an understanding of Nibbana beyond common views to develop an understanding of a Stream Winner.

May all of the noble wishes of those who read this book and practice Dhamma diligently be fulfilled, and may all beings be well and happy.

Chapter One

DHAMMA: STREAM ENTRY

When Dhamma is understood, it is of benefit to those who practice Dhamma. When Dhamma is misunderstood, it produces no benefit to those who practice Dhamma. Although the term "Dhamma" is used in many ways by ordinary people[1], Dhamma itself means Stream Entry (Sotapanna) and other three stages of enlightenment.

In contemporary times, it is most common to hear about Dhamma as divisions or from ordinary disciples who are yet to develop a deep understanding of Dhamma for themselves. Ordinary views of Dhamma and various kinds of ordinary views, including clinging to divisions, language, or things that are not directly related to Dhamma practice are commonly heard and are available for people across societies.

The teachings beyond ordinary views of Dhamma are rare, and those who wish to pursue the disciple route (noble Sangha) to reach a Stream Entry and gain benefit for themselves will need

---

[1] The term ordinary person is referring to indicate common practitioners, it is simply used for the purpose of clarifying the relevant matter without an intention to make differential treatment towards anyone.

to reflect wisely and understand the teachings beyond ordinary views.

Teachings leading to Nibbana can be developed based on developing the right understanding of the deep teachings. To move beyond an ordinary person to become a noble person, gaining a deeper understanding of the teachings are needed and other external factors are not applicable.

To develop the deep understanding of the teachings of Buddha leading to Nibbana, there is a need to go beyond ordinary views to gain noble views and go beyond ordinary techniques to train in the noble techniques; in doing so to develop factors of Stream-entry and develop a mental state of a Stream-enterer.

Below are some of the common questions that are related to Nibbana:

What is (Cessation) Nibbana?

Nibbana that is universally applicable through Noble Sangha route includes four stages, and it begins with the stage of Stream Entry and ends with the stage of Arahantship.

Why is Nibbana a Universal Truth?

Nibbana is functioning at the universal level, just like a birth for beings. Therefore, social level functioning and practices alone are not sufficient to gain benefits of a Dhamma practice and social identities, and divisions are not relevant for gaining the mind state of a Stream-enterer.

Why Truth?

The Dhamma practice leading to Nibbana is based on truth. If one genuinely becomes truthful to one's practice, meaning paying respect and homage to Buddha and his teachings genuinely in one's mind without desire for self-gain, whether it be material, honor, or various other gains, one will be able to gain fruition. Otherwise, despite years of practice, one is unlikely to gain benefits of one's practice meaning Sotapanna and above.

Essentially, we are referring to what's in one's mind and intention. So, for example, if we were to use common words, it may be that someone chooses to live the lifestyle of a monk based on rituals but has too many desires for gain for oneself and to promote oneself. Such behaviour indicates a decline in the purity of the mind and a lack of respect towards Buddha and his teachings, as one who truly respects Buddha will want to develop inner qualities similar to him. This can be said with reference to someone choose to live the lifestyle of a householder, who may engage in unwholesome activities despite knowing the theory and having too many desires for self-gain and a tendency to discriminate against others. On many grounds, this will indicate a lack of purity of the mind and a lack of respect towards the Buddha who has shown the path. Thus, the training path is based on merits and respect. One who respects Buddha wants to develop higher wisdom and maintain similar qualities internally. Imitating, dressing or acting like an Arahant is not the same as developing true inner qualities, this is because imitating will not abandon sufferings and Samsara. Dressing up and making an act without developing higher wisdom and inner qualities will not bring benefits to the practitioners. Thus, in noble path, priority is given to developing higher wisdom and inner qualities. Thus, the practice depends on one's true practice in the heart, which shapes one's mental states, karma and merits.

Who is Buddha?

Prince Siddhartha Gautama born in Nepal became a Supreme Buddha and it's been around 2,500 years ago.

Buddhahood and Arahantship, are they two different routes?

Buddha himself was an Arahant, the first Arahant of our times and those who follow noble Sangha route or those who wish to become a future Buddha, they all will be an Arahant meaning someone who has abandoned greed, hate and delusion.

Difference between Buddhahood and Arahantship though disciple route is that Buddha understands for himself and establish a Sasana and all other arahants are the followers of Buddha.

What is Triple Gem?

Triple Gem indicates Buddha, his teachings leading to Nibbana and his enlightened disciples irrespective of tradition or schools.

The Triple Gem remains the same for all practitioners despite socially created divisions.

Who are noble disciples or noble Sangha?

Noble disciples are the ones who have attained enlightenment and they are four types (those who have attained Sotapanna, Sakadagami, Anagami and Arahant). The noble Sangha (as in the Triple Gem) means the noble people who have experienced enlightenment and are freed from self-view, doubts about Buddha and his teachings and are practicing Dhamma in the correct way.

All Arahants have the same understanding of Dhamma and having directly known, they will teach the same Dhamma following the ancient training path beyond common ways. By understanding true Dhamma leading to Nibbana or liberation, one can eliminate all stress and sufferings if one aspires for it.

Essentially, upon attaining enlightenment, one develops confidence in the Buddha, Dhamma, and noble Sangha and an individual comes to realize through direct knowledge that Buddha is the worthy One, the Perfect Sambuddha, the one who understands the world and the teacher of Gods and men. Similarly, noble disciples come to realize through direct knowledge that the Dhamma has been well-proclaimed by the Buddha.

Who are disciples or Sangha?

Sangha is a community of friends. Noble friends or Sangha and other friends who are still practicing to becoming noble belong together, as they intend to follow the teachings of the same teacher, Buddha.

Friends who follow the teachings may carry different levels of deep understanding of the teachings of Buddha depending on their level of attainment across four stages of enlightenment or whether they have reached a noble state or are ordinary and are still practicing becoming a noble person. Sangha meant to look after one another, and all. The entire practice leading to Nibbana depend on noble friendship.

What is a worlding and a noble disciple?

There is a difference between worlding and a noble disciple, regarding understanding deep Dhamma across fourfold Nibbana and inner qualities; they function in different ways.

Before entering the Noble Eightfold Path, one's mind tend to be focused on worldly matters, and functions in a worldly matter that they have desire to experience or not to experience due to identity view or tendency to identifying things may it be pleasures or displeasures. Similarly, the reason for liking pleasures and disliking displeasures happens when there is a strong grasp of identify view "I". Although it is a general tendency of beings liking to experience good things and avoiding bad things, things on earth are always changing and both pleasures and displeasures are a part of life, and by understanding this universally applicable truth, noble disciples develop disenchanting to experience desires and not experiencing desires and become disenchanted to worldly matters at Arahantship. The middle way practice means abandoning the desires and not having desires for experiencing likes and dislikes. An Arahant means someone who is not restricted in thoughts, for example, it is not about wanting to follow a particular religion, division, or a lifestyle but become free of such things and grasping and giving too much value to such things in mind, free of desire to experience things and desire to not experience things, it is in this manner one can be free of mind made world.

Why doubts?

Unless one sees for oneself, one will not completely understand what Nibbana is, and, therefore, one will possess doubts, which may cause one to possess various views that contradict the teachings of Buddha leading to Nibbana.

What can be done to abandon doubts?

Given that understanding is a subjective process, subjective understanding of an ordinary person and a noble person differs, subjective understanding can be developed by hearing Dhamma (Dhamma meaning Arahantship) from someone who has completed four-fold Nibbana, as unless one has completed the training across four stages of Nibbana, it is unlikely that one will comprehend Nibbana fully.

Thus, entire Dhamma path leading to Nibbana depend on noble friendship. It is of great importance to hear the teachings of Buddha from a noble one such as an Arahant, someone who has completed and understood four stages of Nibbana, a state of mind that can be seen as a safe haven in which there will be no more great future suffering and liberation will follow with certainty.

What about various practices and divisions?

One of the ordinary view, miscomprehensions regarding the practice leading to Nibbana is thinking there are various ways of practicing or training to Nibbana based on socially created divisions. One example is thinking that the way of practicing Dhamma can differ based on one's geographical location. Let's say, for example, that there are 195 countries that have been created based on social identities in the world, and, sometimes, we can see practitioners tend to divide and identify the teachings of Buddha based on the countries in which they live. They cling to their geographical location, because they give too much value to their self-identify or self-view and to identifying self (or body) belonging to a particular geographical location. When they try to explain the practice leading to Nibbana, they come up with different views with an underlying tendency to identify and cling, which prevents them from entering into Nibbana for themselves and others.

The need to divide the teachings comes due to grasping to identity views, and self-view. Unless they lessen their grasping identity views, their mind will not learn to live without grasping. The same is true for other identities, may they be lifestyle, gender, age, divisions, and giving too much value to such identities in one's mind. By recognizing the consequences, practitioners will need to mindfully abandon this to practice their mind in a way that will lead to abandoning fetters and to training the mind to Nibbana.

What about textbooks?

Books are written materials that can be used to develop understanding of Dhamma. Yet, the training ways, and the easiest way to develop higher knowledge leading to Arahantship can be developed by hearing or providing an opportunity to hear the teachings of Buddha that lead to Stream Entry from someone who has gained to such an understanding. Therefore, it was decided not to write Dhamma in books during Buddha's times because hearing Dhamma from Arahants would facilitate gaining an understanding of Nibbana in the right manner. Understanding deep Dhamma is all that is needed for developing the way of practice and noble path, with the arising of right view, one discerns wrong view, and in doing so, when a person has right view, he or she undertakes right resolve, right speech, right action, right livelihood, right effort, right mindfulness, and right concentration. This is how from right view comes success in the training path leading to Nibbana across stages.

Similarly, depending on whether the content of a particular book is coming from someone who has gained a full knowledge of Dhamma or someone who has yet to gain Nibbana, the ability of a book to explain deep Dhamma across four-fold Nibbana may differ. For example, even some of the oldest books written by certain authors indicate no sign that the authors who wrote the books have gained four-fold Nibbana before writing them, and, not knowing Nibbana, they would have tended to express ordinary views in their books.

Similarly, one can only explain Dhamma within one's knowledge level. In some of the oldest sources, let's say for example, Pali Canon, someone with an ordinary understanding can only explain Suttas within their level of understanding. A Sotapanna can explain the Suttas within their Sotapanna level of Dhamma knowledge, a Sakadagami can explain the same Suttas within their Sakadagami level of Dhamma knowledge, an Anagami can explain the same Suttas within their Anagami level of Dhamma knowledge, and an Arahant can explain the same Suttas with highest knowledge.

Arahants are rare. Over centuries, in the absence of Arahants, books have been used as tools to facilitate readers in developing Dhamma knowledge. However, as mentioned above, textbooks are not Nibbana, as Nibbana is a natural process that happens in one's mind and can be found among those who have gained such a state.

While some books can explain Nibbana better than others, anyone who practices the teachings in a right manner will gain benefits or fruition of their Dhamma practice. Four-fold Nibbana goes beyond what can be commonly found in books and similar sources. Similarly, textbooks are creations of society, while Nibbana is a universal function applicable to all. Therefore, divisions based on textbooks are not applicable to Nibbana.

Before gaining to Stream Entry, it may be useful to read books on the teachings and gain some preliminary understanding. However, reading books and understanding the teachings in common ways alone is not sufficient to develop a vision of a

Stream Winner. To gain Nibbana, there is a need to go beyond common ways.

Why there are many ordinary views?

It appears that the practice leading to Nibbana is interpreted in many ways across societies. The reason why many views exist regarding Dhamma practice including divisions is simply due to the fact that ordinary people have differing understandings of Dhamma. Nevertheless, the deep understanding of Dhamma among noble people does not differ (except for their level of attainment) but remains the same, and those who have gained understanding up to Arahantship for themselves can explain the training to others with reasons.

The Training Path that leads to Nibbana contains different levels of progress, different levels of attainments. Given that it is not possible to fully comprehend the Sotapanna state before one gains such a state, and a Sotappana is unable to fully comprehend the Sakadagami state, and not knowing what four-fold Nibbana is, ordinary views regarding Dhamma and the practice vary and are many. Yet, all Arahants (from the past, present and the future), they understand the same training path and the way of training the mind.

If a person does not gain a deep understanding of Dhamma, it is unreasonable to expect that the person can explain the training path (or the Dhamma leading to Nibbana) to another, as it would be saying without knowing, and explaining the training path to Nibbana without knowing is an irresponsible act. Such an act can mislead and prevent Nibbana for others or those who seek it. This is why it was decided not to write Dhamma in books but share orally during Buddha's stime, and it was normal to declare attainment of enlightenment during Buddha's time so that they could explain the practice to others, and those who have truly attained such a state declare such attainment without bringing themselves in to the picture, without an ego or desire to gain for themselves but simply for others to gain.

Therefore, the practice described by an ordinary person is not the same as the practice clarified by a noble disciple or friend, and the path leading to Nibbana depends on noble friends or noble Sangha, who are genuinely caring nice people, who avoid mistreating others on any ground in practice. For example, a person can know the theoretical aspects and what's in books and possess years of mediative experience or live a certain life style, yet if all of these have been performed without developing higher wisdom (Arahatship) (respect towards Triple Gem and abandoning desires for gaining for oneself, as it is self-view that needs abandoning), as all of these things can be done without necessarily developing higher wisdom and inner qualities. A wrong training path can prevent others from gaining Nibbana, as for centuries, it is rare to find noble ones, and those who have gained the right understanding, declaring and sharing their understanding with others and without any discrimination and desires, which is a noble act.-The noble way of thinking and principle that is applied here is when one has something to offer to another. It can be offered without desires and with genuine care and loving kindness toward others.

What is noble ordination?

Ordinary understanding is that social ordination is the ordination in the lineage of Buddhas. To train to cessation, giving up in mind refers to giving up getting attached to one's thoughts that make up the presence of materials, the world, self-view, and others in one's mind. In other words, whatever material things that are physically present and whatever the world is physically present should not interfere with one's mind. Thus, in line with noble standards, whoever maintains mental detachment and not getting attached to their thoughts, and who has abandoned greed, hate, and delusions to various degrees across four stages are noble disciples of Buddha; ordination in the noble lineage indicates meeting with Buddha and his teachings directly in one's heart and gaining a deeper understanding of the teachings to abandon greed, hate and delusion. This can be achieved by cleansing the mind through proper techniques.

What about precepts/training rules?

One of the common or ordinary views is that precepts or training rules are the foundation of stream entry and beyond. Virtues as precepts are a useful practice, however, there is a need to go beyond virtues to develop the right knowledge and gain a deeper understanding of the teachings to reach a mind of a stream enter. It is beneficial to lay a foundation of moral disciplines but moral disciple without developing deep understanding of a steam enterer is not sufficient to gain a mind state of a stream enterer. Upon attaining the first stage of enlightenment, one will naturally behave with morals due to insight without needing to observe precepts as rules. That is to say, there is a need to go beyond common precepts to develop noble virtues.

To go beyond commonly practiced virtues to gain Stream Entry, practicing noble precepts (abstain from killing living beings, stealing, sexual misconduct, false speech, backbiting, harsh or abusive speech, useless or meaningless conversation, wrong means of livelihood) , becoming a good person who looks after others as applicable to oneself (it may be looking after friends, family, an employer or employees, ascetics and so forth), and becoming an ethical person who genuinely cares for others and avoids discriminating against others on any grounds is the practice that is helpful in developing noble virtues, a factor of stream entry.

Sometimes, we can see even among those who have not heard of Dhamma and do not know much about Dhamma that they are good people who care for others, do not show differential treatments towards others, or discriminate against others. In contrast, sometimes we can see that those who know the theoretical aspects of Dhamma and spend hours mediating can still show differential treatment towards others, discriminate against others or cling to identities of various kinds. Impartiality applied in situations, not discriminating against others is a component of practice required to develop noble virtues, which is why it is important to develop beyond precepts or training rules to treat everyone with genuine loving kindness and care. Similarly, giving and sharing materials, knowledge and similar things with others, caring towards others and fulfilling responsibilities towards others is an aspect of the practice that leads to Nibbana, and, unless one genuinely develops these qualities internally, the time and effort spent on practicing Dhamma will bear no benefit in the long run. When it is possible to experience blissful Nibbana, they will continue in samsara due to not understanding the practice and applying the understanding into their practice.

How can one abandon fetters?

Across fourfold Nibbana, there are ten fetters. The fetters can be abandoned by developing middle way training in mind . The Sotapanna will abandon the three fetters of self-illusion, uncertainty, and clinging to mere rules and ritual. The Sakadagami will mitigate lust, hatred, and delusion. The Anagami will eradicate the fetters of sensual lust and ill will. The Arahant will eradicate five more fetters, namely, attachment to fine-material existence, attachment to immaterial existence, conceit, restlessness, and ignorance.

Regarding the practice of abandoning the relevant fetters, one can train to abandon a non-self-view (rites, and rituals, and doubts) by training the mind in the middle way in daily life. For example, by understanding that life is impermanent and that ups and downs are part of life for all of us and are universally applicable to all beings, one can train the mind not to become disheartened when faced with bad events and, similarly, not to become overjoyed when experiencing good events, as they do not last long, and, in doing so, train the mind in the middle way in daily life (middle mind training is given up at the arahant state to lead to cessation; until then, middle mind training is useful). Regarding doubts, to become a noble person or an enlightened disciple of Buddha, rites and rituals, ceremonies, schools and traditions, external factors (gender, age, appearance, nationality etc.) are not relevant, but one's level of gaining a deeper understanding of the stages of Nibbana (or attainment of Nibbana) and the extent of abandoning greed, hate and delusion is what applies. Given that Nibbana happens naturally shaped by Karma and merits, anyone anywhere practicing the teachings in a right manner will be able to gain fruition.

What about loving kindness meditation?

Loving-kindness meditation is one of the popular meditation practices. Although beginners may continue to practice loving-kindness as a form of meditation limiting the practice to a comfortable time (may it be 15 minutes, 30 minutes per day or hours based on personal preference), to gain in to Stream Entry, one needs to establish their mindfulness and concentrate in the Triple Gem, entry point to Stream Entry. For those who wish to gain Nibbana, should they wish to practice loving-kindness meditation, it will be useful to develop and practice loving-kindness along with developing four factors of Stream Entry; becoming a good person by abandoning pride, hate and similar things while developing noble virtues, engage in meritorious activities and attending to Triple Gem, reflecting the qualities of Triple Gem and abandoning fetters, as otherwise, loving-kindness meditation alone will be insufficient to gaining Stream Entry.

The teachings leading to Nibbana are based on the right understanding, upon gaining the right view (right view is gained at the first stage of enlightenment, i.e. Sotapanna) one will not be reborn but will attain full enlightenment by becoming an Arahant at a random instance depending on one's own karma and merits. Along with the right view gained (the right view is gained by attaining the first stage of enlightenment at the Sotapanna stage), if one continues to maintain loving-kindness in daily life and throughout waking hours, this practice will help one eliminate ill will along with sensual desires at the Anagami state and to become an Arahant. In practice, by combining the right view (developing four factors of stream entry, abandoning the fetters) to loving-kindness practice in daily life, one will be able to progress in the path of enlightenment.

What about mindfulness meditation?

One of the common or ordinary views is that the technique to gain realization is living in the present moment and being aware. However, to gain realization, there is a need to go beyond commonly used techniques to developing four factors of stream-entry and abandoning the relevant fetters.

Momentary awareness is maintained through conscious efforts, which is how the ordinary understanding of Dhamma can be interrupted and may be unlikely to be stable. This explains why, for an ordinary person, there is continued existence (Samsara). However, if maintaining momentary awareness as a meditation practice can be supported by the Triple Gem to generate merits (giving, reflecting, or mediating the qualities of the Triple Gem, and developing noble virtues indicates looking after others as applicable to oneself and avoiding discriminating against others on many grounds), in a way leading to developing four factors of stream-entry and abandoning fetters (develop middle mind training in daily life within one's lifestyle to abandon self-view and abandon clinging to divisions, ceremonies, rites, and rituals), such a noble practice will lead to gaining blissful Nibbana.

What about sensual desires?

Sensual desires refer to desires come from five senses.

At the third stage of enlightenment, one eliminates sensual desires and ill will at the same time. This happens naturally during the process of enlightenment, when one gains the insight of non-self-view that drives one towards the higher stages of enlightenment naturally due to insight. Therefore, one who aspire to achieve enlightenment requires to eliminate self-view first. As a consequence of understanding non-self-view, the rest nine things will be naturally eradicated in an individual's mind, and the path to enlightenment will become a comfortable middle way.

What about jhanas?

When an individual practice in line with Buddha's teaching, typically, one will experience jhanas after attaining the Anagami stage (with removal of two fetters: sensual desires and ill will) and essentially after removing the three fetters at the Sotapanna stage (i.e self-view, doubts about Buddha, Dhamma and Sangha, attachment for rites, and rituals). Jhanas are needed to gain the higher stages of enlightenment (Arahantship) but in reality, jhanas are not developed as consciously developed meditation practice, rather jhanas come to establish naturally in the mind of a practitioner at a random instance once after one completed Anagami state followed by insight of non-self-view gained at the Sotapanna level, and it is a happening like birth for beings, and not a conscious process of meditation as the practice that is typically done and seen among ordinary friends.

Jhana or the concentrative state would come under the right concentration, which is the eighth factor in the Noble Eightfold Path, should accompany by the right view, and that is to say, noble path always begins with right understanding of deep Dhamma & Triple Gem. What needs to be done to gain Nibbana is developing understanding.

Typically, Arahants can enter into states of absorption (jhanas) at any time they wish and also experience "Nirodha Samapatti" (cessation). Nibbana brings stability, and jhanas are temporary states, and from that perspective, Nibbana is a blissful state than remaining in a state of jhanas. Nibbana is experienced at four stages (Sotapanna, Sakadagami, Anagami and Arahant).

An individual who attains the stage of Sotapanna will certainly achieve Arahatship at some point, although time may vary between individuals (it can happen within the very next moment to next day or next year to a maximum of 7 births).

Thus, for those who are interested in achieving enlightenment, it will be beneficial to put extra effort to achieve the stage of Sotapanna.

What is the change of linage and birth in noble linage?

Stream-entry is a state of mind that occurs when the practitioner has understood the teachings of Buddha to abandon doubts about what Buddha taught. Having a comprehension of Buddha's teachings, a stream enterer eradicates three fetters at once: clinging to self-view, precepts, and traditions including rites and rituals. This is because at the heart of the teachings of Buddha is a practice that is genuine to one's heart. Therefore, a practitioner at this stage will no longer validate the need to cling to precepts or rites and rituals but will be liberated from such bindings to experience peace and freedom within. It is called "Stream-entry", because one enters the stream, Buddha's training path leading to higher attainments that lies beyond ordinary ways. When entering the stream, a change of linage takes place in that one comes to belong to the noble linage of Buddha due to a transition that happens in one's mind from the state of an ordinary being to becoming a noble being who possesses a noble character. This process happens out of rites and rituals meaning that any person from any background can come to belong to a noble Sangha by entering the Stream-entry state in one's mind. Thus, external factors and social practices do not have an impact, for example, someone practicing a monk lifestyle (ritualistically) and someone living the lifestyle of a householder have an opportunity to become a noble Sangha by transitioning from an ordinary being to a noble being in the path leading to Arahathship, the highest stage of noble sainthood. Listening to Dhamma from a person who has attained enlightenment (a noble person) is helpful to developing the right vision. This is because noble people can share their direct experiences and explain the direct way of training the mind to gain Nibbana. One can attain enlightenment by paying careful attention to Dhamma as described by an Arahant and practicing in line with Buddha's teaching.

Ordinary understanding is that social ordination is the ordination in the lineage of Buddhas. In line with noble standards, whoever maintains mental detachment, and who has abandoned greed, hate, and delusions to various degrees across four stages are noble disciples of Buddha; ordination in the noble lineage indicates meeting with Buddha and his teachings directly in one's heart and gaining a deeper understanding of the teachings to abandon greed, hate and delusion. This can be achieved by cleansing the mind through proper techniques (Reflecting the qualities of the Triple Gem and attending to the Triple Gem).

What is the role of social practices in Nibbana?

Nibbana is a universal happening shaped by karma and merits. Social practices are not relevant and not of much importance, as social practices alone cannot shape one's karma, and social practices alone cannot enhance one's internal qualities. It is easy to perform a ritual, but it may be difficult to develop inner qualities. For example, someone can commit various kinds of unwholesome things to a perform ritual, but just by performing a ritual, such a person is unable to abandon unwholesome qualities or develop merits that replace unwholesome qualities. Thus, developing internal qualities leads to the mind state of a stream enterer.

Can Nibbana be consciously produced and entered by force??

It is not possible to enter Nibbana by force as one's ability to gain Nibbana is shaped by one's karma and merits, thus, it is not a consciously produced state or conscious maintenance of mindfulness, rather, Nibbana is a happening, because it happens at a random instance just like birth for beings.

Nibbana is four-fold. Achieving Nibbana across four stages can be considered the most important step in one's life and samsara because Nibbana abandons future births and deaths and sufferings that come along with life, the birth and death of beings. One's ability to gain Nibbana is shaped by one's karma. This is to say that Nibbana is a natural process just like the birth and death of beings; it happens on its own time shaped by karmic influence.

Chapter Two

NIBBANA: A BIRTH IN NOBLE LINAGE

Stream Entry is not a consciously produced state but a natural process that happens in a random instance just like birth for beings. That moment allows a being to be born in the noble linage and brings stable change in a being so that a person who was before stream entry will not be the one after stream entry. A person who becomes a Stream Winner comes to possess good inner qualities in an instant. What he or she used to be before such a state of entry can no longer be found internally. For example, a drunkard can be changed in an instant never to drink excessively again; a thief can be changed to a person who never steals again; a person who used to be so sad every day will not be so sad again.

Given that Nibbana happens across four stages, it can be said it is a progressive process. However, each state can happen in an instant or in a few moments of time. For example, stream entry happens in a moment of time and may continue through a few moments, but a stream enterer is unable to sustain the same thoughts for a longer period of time and retain other fetters.

Due to retaining fetters, each stage of Nibbana and the relevant mind states differ, and so the state of a stream entry is different from a state of the mind of an Arahant.

It takes a single moment of time to become a Sakadagami, An Arahant state may take several moments of time, as the mind goes into various kinds of Jhanas. It is a natural process and not what is commonly known as sitting, meditating and gaining concentration. Rather, it is a process that can happen instantly and naturally at a random instance after Stream Entry.

Although Nibbana across four stages is a progressive process, each stage happens in its own time, and each stage happens very fast. The state of Stream Entry and Sotapanna happen in a moment of time, and the Sotapanna state that happens in one's thoughts will last a few moments. But, because a Sotapanna is unable to sustain such thoughts day and night, Sotapanna remains bonded to sense desires and higher fetters. Thus, practice leading to Nibbana is not a conscious maintenance of a thought process. Rather, because of developing merits, the thoughts come maintain a non-self view and let go of stability. Therefore, merits play a key role here.

In sum, Nibbana is fruition that is established in one's mind due to the right practice of Dhamma. It is a training in mind that applies not other factors.

Nibbana is four-fold, and the practices that lead to each of these stages of Nibbana differ. Those who practice the teachings in the right way in a manner that leads to stream-entry will be able to attain Nibbana.

Chapter Three

BEYOND ORDINARY VIEWS: EGO, PRIDE, AND LIFESTYLE

The path that leads to Nibbana is based on universally applicable karma, and everyone who has fulfilled the requirement of merits for gaining Stream Entry, influenced by their karma, can gain a state of Stream Entry at a random instance. In other words, when they get to hear teachings leading to Nibbana, they will want to listen, and their own karma will make it possible for them to make sense of teachings beyond ordinary views when they get to hear such teachings from noble ones. Otherwise, even if the message is readily available, they will be unable to recognize and make sense of the teachings, and, eventually, their own karma will shape their ability to gain Nibbana.

Birth in Nobel linage happens at a random instance just like birth for beings out of socially created rites and rituals. Thus, Nibbana is not about a lifestyle that is created and accepted by social standards but a happening at a universal level like birth for beings.

Societies that are created based on ordinary standards and noble standards are not the same. To abandon fetters, the practice requires training the mind to understand beyond ordinary ways "against the current ways of thinking and doing" (patisotagamini). For example, ordinary ways of thinking, such as "positive thinking" or "negative thinking" when things change, can generate stress. Instead, reverse thinking or thinking beyond ordinary ways in a middle way requires, for example, "if something works, it is good", "if something does not work, it's still ok and good, and in that case, I will find practical solutions," and these kinds of middle way thinking must be applied to daily life. Similarly, the kind of expectations a person has for example, "others will care and that they will look after me", "I will be successful in the tasks I do", and the kind of expectations that others create, and the society create from the time a person grows up; "you can own a house, a family, a good job when you grow up" and similar things, and when such expectations do not come to be fulfilled in life, and similar things, people get disappointed, and depressed and can develop suicidal thoughts in daily life. Yet, the Dhamma vision means that understanding anything is possible in life for all of us and applying thoughts that "let whatever happen but I will do what I can do to my best, if something works that's great but if not, that's still ok I will find an alternative way", and similar thoughts, if applied in daily life can take off excessive stress away from a person. If these kinds of thinking are applied to daily life, they will be useful for everyone, for students in schools and universities, employees and employers, families, and for the whole of society, and some of the problems, such as mental health problems, can be resolved to a greater extent, as the way of thinking can lead to developing depression and similar things, and these things can be avoided by applying healthy thinking. However, developing thinking alone is not Nibbana; it is just a way of training the middle mind.

Based on ordinary understanding, the techniques to gain insight or super-seeing (vipassana) indicates living in the present moment and letting go. A noble understanding of insight development indicates developing the right view of a Stream Enterer, an entry point of gaining a deeper understanding of the Triple Gem to develop four factors of Stream-entry and abandoning three fetters by understanding the deep Dhamma taught by Buddha. The noble view of vipassana indicates Sotapanna, Sakadagami, Anagami and Arahant.

Subject to individual differences, an ordinary person may acknowledge someone else's teachings as the teachings of Buddha or mix up various other subjects into Dhamma. For example, lacking a full understanding of what Nibbana is, some practitioners mix up various other subjects (e.g. gender issues, society issues, economic political issues, and language such as Pali or Sanskrit) and spend their time talking about things that are not directly relevant to gaining Nibbana. In doing so, a person engages in doing things that are not part of a practice that allows one to train one's mind in a way leading to Nibbana, for example, it be may that some practitioners despite they are saying that they are following precepts or training rules, if they will spend a lot of time boasting self; discussing their academic achievements, conferences they visited, and about their students/families/political issues during the time that is allocated for Dhamma activities such as a Dhamma talk, and in doing so, they fail to maintain noble precepts; avoiding meaningless conversations. When a person's mind receives no enough training, a person may not be able to abandon a strong sense of self-view, and a person's mind will have a tendency to cling to various divisions, and the tendency in a mind of grasping to self-view can be expressed in a person's speech. A person may divide the teachings based on division and geographical locations, unless give up dividing and clinging to divisions, such practices can prevent Nibbana for a person. This happens because a person is still ordinary and is yet to understand Dhamma practice, which is universally applicable to gaining Nibbana.

While doing other things, and applying Dhamma in daily life, a wise person should be able to develop higher knowledge (Arahantship). For example, ideally, a person should be able to develop Dhamma practice while studying other subjects as separate subject matters and going on doing other things in life. However, given that Dhamma is unique, if a person will mix up Dhamma by adding things that are not taught by Buddha into Dhamma, such a practice can delay or prevent Nibbana for a person. This is because to gain a vision of a Stream Winner requires gaining a precise knowledge of what Buddha has said and taught and the correct way of practice leading to Nibbana.

In general, the word "venerable" is used in societies to address those who live a ritualistic lifestyle, while those who write books about Dhamma, carry theoretical knowledge and can be seen as venerable for their contribution. Similarly, others in different fields, such as engineering, science, or medicine, can be venerable for their contributions to their fields. For example, good parents can be venerable for looking after their children, and if applied noble standards of not treating others differently, equally to everyone, a person who cleans a street, be seen as venerable if the person is honest, hardworking and contributes to maintaining clean streets. Similarly, a homeless person can be seen as venerable if the person possesses good inner qualities, higher wisdom. To gain Stream Entry, developing noble virtues require one to develop higher wisdom and inner qualities similar to Buddha, therefore, not treating others differentially is essential for developing noble virtues beyond precepts and to progress in noble path.

The usage of venerable and arahant are not the same, as arahant was originally used during Buddha's time to refer to someone who has completed fourfold Nibbana from any background, and background (country, age, gender, etc.) does not impact

Nibbana. They are freed from greed (getting attached to thoughts that create view of me, myself and others and such views and desires for gains for oneself), hate (me, myself and others and such views and disliking and intending to cause discomfort to others) and delusion (me, myself, and others and such views, and pride that comes with such views and the need to divide teachings and others; religion, Buddhism, tradition, life style, men and women, etc.). Having abandoned fetters, Arahant means that they do not keep secrets or keep teachings a secret, as they share the teachings without merely keeping their knowledge and attainment for themselves without an ego in a humble manner, simply because sharing the highest knowledge can benefit others, and they can also provide higher merits to others.

It seems that, in societies that function in common ways, most practitioners don't talk about their attainment. Consequently, it is reasonable to assume that they have not attained to Nibbana, as, otherwise, Nibbana is typically a self-declaration, and declaration should always accompany reasoning, so that, as Buddha did, they should explain teachings without desiring to gain for themselves. First, unless people have gained Nibbana, it is reasonable to accept that they are unlikely to know what fourfold Nibbana is, they will not know beyond ordinary views, and they will possess only theoretical knowledge. Thus, all those who practice Dhamma, if they will apply Dhamma for their own practice, they will be humble and honest to take the responsibility to self-declare their attainment before sharing Dhamma with others. Ordinary friends can share Dhamma knowledge at the ordinary level, a Soatapanna can share Dhamma knowledge at the Sotapanna level, a Sakadagami can share Dhamma knowledge at the Sakadagami level, an Anagami can share Dhamma knowledge at Anagami level, an Arahant can share Dhamma knowledge to the Arahant level. In noble linage, one's Attainment is declared simply for providing knowledge and merits to others but not to gain benefits for self, or to show differential treatment for others. Ordinary Sangha or community of practitioners can still discuss theoretical aspects of Dhamma, contribute to Dhamma in whatever the way they can by acknowledging that they are yet to gain a noble state, and they can still gain benefits, such as materials, that are needed for their survival, and continuing in their own practice, share what they possess, knowledge, materials and similar things with others, in that manner, Dhamma across four-fold Nibbana can be made visible and available for the benefit for all. As a result, ordinary Sangha communities will have more chances in developing into noble communities.

As we know, even among ordinary people Dhamma knowledge and inner qualities differ. Similarly, one who maintains precepts and training rules may find their precepts can sometimes change but those who have gained noble virtues will be unlikely to experience instability, as noble virtues remain stable in those who possess such virtues, and they will be free of sufferings, and Samsara. A Stream Winner can expect to give up continuous death and birth process, suffering, and Samsara. Gaining a clear comprehension of deep Dhamma across fourfold Nibbana will bring benefit to those who wish to give up suffering, and samsara.

The training path leading to Nibbana is based on understanding deep Dhamma (right vision, is where noble eight-fold begins). With regard to Dhamma, wrong understanding refers to not understanding Karma, and understanding of Dhamma should come at different levels.

Understanding of deep Dhamma of an ordinary person is not the same understanding of a Stream Winner. The purpose of the noble order is to share higher wisdom and provide merit to others. In comparison to a Soatapanna, an ordinary practitioner has less capacity to provide wisdom and merits to others, a Sakadagami possesses more ability to provide wisdom and merits to others if compared to a Sotapanna, an Anagami possesses more capacity to provide wisdom and merits to others comparable to a Sakadagami, an Arahant possesses the highest capacity. Even at Anagami state, one needs merits and guidance to develop further, the purpose of noble friends is to support and look after one another and all. Thus, hearing Dhamma from someone who has completed full training across four stages and by receiving merits that can be gained by attending to them is helpful for all practitioners to gain Nibbana, a practice that is universally applicable for all.

Sometimes, we hear some practitioners based on their ordinary view say that they don't declare their attainment, as declaring can make someone proud. Yet, such a statement contradicts Dhamma. For example, while it may be possible for an ordinary person to experience pride, even for things that are minor, such that, when earning a degree, getting a job, becoming a teacher of a group of students, and other similar things, and due to getting attached to such thoughts, they may have a tendency to experience delight in such things and non-delight in certain other things. This may be applicable to all people around the world, as they follow the standard way of thinking and doing. However, those who think beyond ordinary thinking by not getting attached to their thoughts will not get attached to their thoughts that make up "self-view", greed, hate and delusion that come from self-view including grasping society and similar things. With grasping comes stress, and abandoning stress requires giving up grasping thoughts across four stages. This is one way to train the mind towards Nibbana. Other aspects require developing merits.

Thus, Nibbana is not a lifestyle and getting attached to any life style can prevent Nibbana, being free of desire "to experience" and desire "not to experience" a life style in mind, but follow whatever life style convenient and feasible for one self, without grasping or giving too much value to such things while developing higher wisdom and inner qualities will benefit practitioners, as life style alone is not sufficient for gaining Nibbana; unless one develops mental detachment; passion and dispassion towards a life style, factors of stream entry, and abandon fetters.

For example, if Nibbana were a lifestyle, given that lifestyle can be temporary and subject to change, Nibbana would indicate something temporary in its effect. But Nibbana is a process, as it brings an end to the birth and death process and samsara. Similarly, if Nibbana were a lifestyle, it would indicate that an end of one's lifestyle would bring an end to Nibbana. For example, if those who live the lifestyle of a monk by following rituals based on social standards later decide voluntarily to give up living that lifestyle or to give up a lifestyle due to natural death, they would give up Nibbana. Yet, Nibbana brings an end to such temporary lifestyles, the birth and death process of beings and samsara. For example, when the first noble disciple, Kondanna Arahant left the monastic lifestyle to live in isolation, the fact that he left the monastic order and lived in isolation did not impact his state of Arahantship, as Arahantship is not a lifestyle. Otherwise, lifestyle can be temporary. If Nibbana were a lifestyle, when one leaves a lifestyle, one should revert back from being an arahant to becoming an ordinary person, yet Arahantship is a cessation of samsara, a universal happening just like birth and death for beings. Thus, socially created lifestyle and similar things are not relevant to gaining Nibbana, but to practicing the training in a right manner and to developing the mind to understand truth beyond ordinary views. In doing so, developing middle mind training, shaping one's karma and merits though right practices are relevant. The practice is universally applicable.

To develop the deep understanding of the teachings of Buddha leading to Nibbana, there is a need to go beyond ordinary views to gain noble views and go beyond ordinary techniques to train in the noble techniques; in doing so to develop factors of stream-entry and develop a mental state of a stream-enterer.

The practice described by an ordinary person is not the same as the practice clarified by a noble disciple or friend, and Triple Gem cannot be replaced in alternative ways, the path leading to Nibbana depends on noble friends or noble Sangha, who are genuinely caring nice people, who avoid mistreating others on any ground in practice.

A person who has gained a deeper understanding of the teaching, an Arahant or a noble disciple of Buddha will understand that the teachings of Buddha leading to Nibbana is unique, and universally applicable. The teachings are universally applicable because the path to Nibbana based on universally applicable law of karma. In noble path, declaring one's attainment is simply for sharing knowledge and merits with others in a humble and gentle manner without desire for gains and similar things, a noble act, the noble way of thinking and principle that is applied here is when one has something to offer to another. It can be offered without desires and with genuine care and loving kindness toward others. For example, it may be that someone has extra skills, physical ability, time, richness, or whatever they can offer to another with genuine intention and care, in a humble manner and without gaining, without pride in self and ego, and without discriminating against others on any ground. The acts of such a person are noble. In contrast, if one possesses certain things greater than others, be caste, money, education and similar things, becoming proud, demanding, and discriminating against others and using such things to make others uncomfortable even to a slight degree or to oppress others is not appropriate for a good person. This is an example of how one can reflect and perform one's actions in developing noble virtues that generate merits. If such good thoughts and deeds performed at the individual level can be applied to the societal level where one takes responsibility for performing one's actions in a noble manner, The society will look after itself and will benefit many, so that the impermanent life that we all have can be lived in a more meaningful manner, generating happiness and benefits for all. From a different perspective, this will also help prevent mental suffering for many so that suicide and depression rates can be reduced in good societies and improve the wellbeing for many.

On the contrary, if one possesses certain things greater than others, becoming proud, demanding, and displaying ego and use of such things to make others uncomfortable even to a slight degree or oppress others, or displaying egoistic behavior is not appropriate for a good person. This is an example of how one can reflect and perform one's actions in developing noble virtues that generate merits, if such good thoughts and deeds performed at the individual level can be applied to the societal level where one takes responsibility for performing one's actions in a noble manner, it will be a society that is looking after itself and will benefit many, so that impermanent life we all have can be lived in a more meaningful manner, generating happiness and benefits for all.

Ideally, one who truly wants to gain Nibbana, and represent Buddha as a disciple should develop higher wisdom and inner qualities similar to that of Buddha, in the noble path, less priority is given to developing external factors or external appearance, and more priority is given to developing inner wisdom and inner qualities, the noble path always lies beyond ordinary training ways.

In sum, true knowledge or correct understanding is the first step towards Nibbana, and easiest way to develop true knowledge is hearing the practice from someone who has completed Nibbana. True knowledge means abandoning non-self-views, clinging to rites and rituals, and abandoning doubts along with possessing four factors of Stream Entry. In practice, it may not be possible to abandon fetters at once. For those who wish to gain Nibbana, it will be of benefit to know how to practice the teachings leading to each stage of enlightenment, as each stage differs, so that practice can lead to gaining fruition. For them, it will be beneficial to hear about the Dhamma leading to Nibbana from someone who has already completed the full training path up to Arahantship.

Chapter Four

TRAINING THE MIND

Nibbana is to be experienced in one's mind, and it cannot be experienced outside one's mind. To train to Cessation, cease to exist or Nibbana, giving up in mind refers to giving up getting attached to one's thoughts that make up the presence of materials, the world, self-view, and others in one's mind. In other words, whatever material things that are physically present and whatever the world is physically present should not interfere with one's mind. Nothing should interfere with one's mind. The mind should be trained to remain unaffected in the very presence of such things, which is how one should train one's mind in a way to give up getting attached to one's thoughts that create a self-view and the world. A person who is training to gain Nibbana should be able to live wherever and with whomever, without getting affected by such things, so that the training in one's mind becomes a practical thing to do while doing other things in life. This is how one should train one's mind in a way reach to cessation, to cease to exist, Nibbana.

Not understanding what Nibbana is, sometimes, practitioners seem to think that Nibbana is a lifestyle, but Nibbana is not a lifestyle because a lifestyle itself is created in one's mind. Similarly, practitioners seem to think that giving up the world means giving up material things. Yet material things are created in one's mind, the world is created in one's mind. Similarly, self-view and others are created in one's mind and in one's thoughts. When the physical presence of certain things does not indicate the presence of such things as permanent in one's mind, or as self, others and the world, when such things are changing, changing things won't cause suffering due to the realization that such things are made up in one's thoughts, within one's mind. In this manner, the realization of Nibbana will bring about a practical person, who does things that are needed for the benefit of others and functional in daily life, while being free of the very same things and everything else and all in one's mind. The practice does not require making changes to a person's preferred lifestyle; a person can continue with the person's usual lifestyle and way of living while training one's mind in way that avoids getting attached to one's thoughts in daily life.

However, training the mind to gain cessation requires training the mind in middle ways, such that getting delight and not getting delight in material possessions, gains, honour, and praise in the and similar things should be abandoned across stages, and ideally, one should train one selve thus: 'I will not delight (or non-delight) in the arisen material possessions, gain, honour, praise, a life style, as such things are subject to change" ; 'I will not think myself as similar, better or worse than others; I will not be too much happy or too much sad over events that are passing by", and similar ways in daily life.

The end goal of Nibbana does not have gain, honor, and similar things for its benefit but freedom from all, a mind that is free from the events that are happening in the world, a mind that remains unaffected by the existence of the physical world.
To get to cessation, the mind has to be trained in a correct manner, and knowing the right practice leading to Stream Entry is beneficial for practitioners, and practitioners should train thus:

"We take precepts and training rules to develop noble virtues (the purpose of maintaining virtue and training rules should be to develop noble virtues); we meditate to develop confirmed confidence in the Triple Gem (the purpose of developing concentration as meditation practice is to develop confirmed confidence in the Triple Gem)", the purpose of any lifestyle should be to develop merits, engage in wholesome activities, the end purpose of training the mind is to gain freedom from precepts, a lifestyle, and mind; giving up getting attached to one's thoughts that create self-view, and others towards the end of noble training path".

The purpose of Buddha's teachings is to experience within one's mind. To develop a deep understanding of the teachings of Buddha leading to Nibbana, there is a need to go beyond ordinary views to gain noble views and go beyond ordinary techniques to train in the noble techniques; in doing so to develop factors of stream-entry; abandon fetters and develop a mental state of a stream-enterer.

How can one develop noble virtues?

At the beginning of one's practice, before reaching a mind state of a stream-enterer, one may take precepts or monastic rules and thereafter develop a higher understanding of Dhamma across four stages.

Before reaching Stream Entry stage, one may purify one's bodily action, verbal action, and mental action by repeatedly reflecting upon them; before conducting any bodily, verbal and mental actions, one may reflect whether such physical, verbal, or mental action one is doing lead to cause pain or harm to self or others, if on reflection, one knows that one's action leads to the affliction of self and others, one should not do such things and engage restraint in the future. On the other hand, if on reflection, if one knows one's physical, verbal and mental actions do not lead to affliction of self and others, one may continue with it, stay joyful and training day and night.

How can one develop confirmed confidence in Triple Gem?

Confirmed confidence in the Triple Gem can be developed by reflecting on the qualities of the Triple Gem day and night; recollect the Tathagata; 'Supreme Gautama Buddha, the Blessed One is worthy and rightly self-awakened, possess perfect and highest knowledge & noble conduct, well-gone, an expert with regard to the world, excellent trainer for those people fit to be instructed, the Teacher of divine & human beings, fully enlightened, understood the path by himself and explained the path to us, and blessed'; recollect Dhamma; 'The Dhamma is well-explained by the Blessed One, those who practice correctly will get to experience Dhamma immediately, applicable for all times and thus, timeless, others can be invited to practice and see for themselves, inviting verification, pertinent, can be realized by those who are wise enough to see beyond ordinary ways', and recollect noble Sangha; 'The noble Sangha of the Blessed One's are the good in their practice, they have practiced Dhamma in a correct manner, they are systematic in their practice, they have practiced correctly, and skilfully and gained realization across four stages; noble Sangha of the blessed ones are the incomparable field of merit for the world.' while walking, standing, sitting, and going about doing other things, and attending to the Triple Gem by giving priority to the Triple Gem in one's mind.

How can one abandon fetters?

One can abandon fetters by middle-way training in one's mind. An aspect of middle-way training of the mind requires not giving too much value to thoughts that bring up and develop various identities and similar things in one's mind but just doing whatever benefit others, a practice that be developed progressively across stages.

Below is a guided reflection that can be applied for abandoning getting attached to one's thoughts that create self-view and develop renunciation in daily life:

Mindfully, I breath in...
Mindfully, I breath out...

Mindfully, I am breathing in long...
Mindfully, I am breathing in long...

Mindfully, I will breathe in sensitive to the entire body...
Mindfully, 'I will breathe out sensitive to the entire body...

Mindfully, I breath experiencing peace in this moment...
Mindfully, I beath out experiencing peace in this moment...

Mindfully, I reflect now:

I can get carried away with delight or non-delight in the past, in the past I did this, in the past, I didn't do this...

I can get carried away with delight or non-delight in the future, in the future I will do this, I will not be able to do this...

I can get carried away with delight or non-delight in the present. Yet, mindfully, I reflect wisely, I should not too much chase after the past as past is gone, I should not place too many expectations or get anxious of the future as future is not arrived yet... Whatever happens now, I should not get too much delight and non-delight in the present, instead, I should learn myself to relax and find peace in the moment.

Mindfully, I breath in...
Mindfully, I breath out...

Mindfully, I am breathing in long...
Mindfully, I am breathing in long...

Mindfully, I will breathe in sensitive to the entire body...
Mindfully, 'I will breathe out sensitive to the entire body...

Mindfully, I breath experiencing peace in this moment...
Mindfully, I beath out experiencing peace in this moment...

Mindfully, I reflect now:

Past experiences, present experiences, and future experiences; friends and family matters, issues related to body, appearance of a body, illnesses, money, job, and financial matters, education-related matters, social matters, political and economic matters, other matters, these things happen over and over again. Events happen in cycles.

It's been years since I've born, I've experienced good and bad times, and if I spend too much time thinking about certain things that are worrying me, making me feel unhappy, upset, anxious, or sad, I spend my time making myself suffer.

Yet, life is short, and I deserve better. I deserve to have some peace in mind.

So, I will learn myself not to worry about the past that is gone mindfully as it's gone. I will learn myself not to get too much anxious about the future because it's not yet come mindfully, I will just relax in this moment mindfully and make the most of the present moment.

Mindfully, I breath in...
Mindfully, I breath out...

Mindfully, I am breathing in long...
Mindfully, I am breathing out long...

Mindfully, I will breathe in sensitive to the entire body...
Mindfully, I will breathe out sensitive to the entire body...

Mindfully, I breath experiencing peace in this moment...
Mindfully, I beath out experiencing peace in this moment...

Mindfully, I reflect now:

People come and people go, time flies, days pass by, my life is short, and this is the nature of life.
Therefore, when I am here, while I am able to do things, I will do what is needed and beneficial for myself and others.
When bad events happen, I will think wisely to understand that bad things are a part of life for all of us, it's just not me who experiences bad things in life.
Both good and bad are a part of life for all people around the world, and there is no point in getting disheartened over things that are not possible to change; when faced with problems in life such as poverty, illnesses, and death, so instead of too much worrying over things, I will just take an action to resolve them if possible, do what I can do to the best, and reflect that realization in life experience is what Dhamma is, I am grateful for Dhamma, and I pay homage to the Triple Gem!

Mindfully, I breath in...
Mindfully, I breath out...

Mindfully, I am breathing in long...

Mindfully, I am breathing out long...

Mindfully, I will breathe in sensitive to the entire body...
Mindfully, 'I will breathe out sensitive to the entire body...

Mindfully, I breath experiencing peace in this moment...
Mindfully, I beath out experiencing peace in this moment...

Mindfully, I reflect now:

When happy events happen, as events come and go, if I will get too much overjoyed by such events, it is possible that the things can suddenly change, if I will get too much delighted in events, my mind will also get into the habit of getting too much non delight when bad events happen. Therefore, I will train my mind not to get too much delight and not to get too much non delight in experiences and events, I will learn myself to face events as they come.

In this manner, by giving up experiencing too much delight and too much non-delight and similar ways, I will learn how to function in day-to-day life, meaning I will just do what is needed, and beneficial while maintaining stable peace in my mind reflecting everything is subject to change.

Let me find peace at this moment.

Mindfully, I breath in...

Mindfully, I breath out...

Mindfully, I am breathing in long...
Mindfully, I am breathing out long...

Mindfully, I will breathe in sensitive to the entire body...
Mindfully, I will breathe out sensitive to the entire body...

Mindfully, I breath experiencing peace in this moment...
Mindfully, I beath out experiencing peace in this moment...

Mindfully, I reflect now:

I will not expect anything from anyone as expecting anything from anyone can bring me disappointment. This way, I will protect myself from worldly things.

Mindfully, I breath in...
Mindfully, I breath out...

Mindfully, I am breathing in long...
Mindfully, I am breathing out long...

Mindfully, I will breathe in sensitive to the entire body...
Mindfully, I will breathe out sensitive to the entire body...

Mindfully, I breath experiencing peace in this moment...
Mindfully, I beath out experiencing peace in this moment...

Mindfully, I reflect now:

(For anger, hatred, pride, and jealousy)
When I feel anger, hatred, pride, and jealousy, I experience some discomfort, a burning sensation inside me, and experiencing such restlessness, burning sensation is not easy, and not worthy, and thus, I suffer alone.

Therefore, to get rid of all kinds of fires that are burning me from inside me, I will let go of all bad thoughts that are hidden inside me for a moment.

I want to become a better person; I will find peace in the moment.

Let me find peace at this moment.

Mindfully, I breath in...
Mindfully, I breath out...

Mindfully, I am breathing in long...
Mindfully, I am breathing out long...

Mindfully, I will breathe in sensitive to the entire body...
Mindfully, I will breathe out sensitive to the entire body...

Mindfully, I breath experiencing peace in this moment...
Mindfully, I beath out experiencing peace in this moment...

Mindfully, I reflect now:

(For ignorance in mind, and thoughts)
Outside things are not bothering me, but sometimes, I don't think enough about myself, and I feel that I ignore myself a lot. By ignoring myself, I suffer...
I feel too much disappointed in myself.
I don't wish to ignore myself, but my thoughts have ignored me a lot, thoughts function on their own, thoughts are not me, thoughts are not myself, thoughts are not mine...
No one else can bother me to the extent my own mind and my thoughts, I let go of such thoughts to find peace in this moment.
If thoughts are not me, I am not to be blamed, I do not need to take the blame as it wasn't me, I try and attend to doing some tasks now...
Let me be free of my thoughts for a moment to find peace in this moment.

Mindfully, I breath in...
Mindfully, I breath out...

Mindfully, I am breathing in long...
Mindfully, I am breathing out long...

Mindfully, I will breathe in sensitive to the entire body...
Mindfully, I will breathe out sensitive to the entire body...

Mindfully, I breath experiencing peace in this moment...
Mindfully, I beath out experiencing peace in this moment...

Mindfully, I reflect now:

I let go of my thoughts that are bothering me and bringing me discomfort, thoughts are not mine, thoughts are not me, thoughts are not myself
I let go of my thoughts that are bothering me and bringing me discomfort, thoughts are not mine, thoughts are not me, thoughts are not myself
I let go of my thoughts that are bothering me and bringing me discomfort, thoughts are not mine, thoughts are not me, thoughts are not myself

Mindfully, I breath in...
Mindfully, I breath out...

Mindfully, I am breathing in long...
Mindfully, I am breathing out long...

Mindfully, I will breathe in sensitive to the entire body...

Mindfully, I will breathe out sensitive to the entire body…

Mindfully, I breath experiencing peace in this moment…
Mindfully, I beath out experiencing peace in this moment…

In this manner, middle way training in mind can be applied in many ways. The benefits of Buddha's teachings are to experience them immediately while living daily life, and Dhamma leads to Nibbana, which teaches how to live a satisfied life within one's lifestyle.

To understand deep Dhamma is to abandon sufferings in mind. To train one's mind to gain Nibbana, one needs to understand beyond ordinary ways, and ordinary ways of identifying Dhamma may include religion, division, rites and rituals, ceremonies, or lifestyle based on social practices. An aspect of middle-way training of mind requires not giving too much value to these identities in mind or clinging to such things.

How can one develop merits?
By reflecting on the qualities of the Triple Gem, and attending to Supreme Buddha, Arahant, Anagami, Sakadagami, Sotapanan in order, engaging in wholesome activities, developing generosity and recollect one's own generosity to amplify merits: 'I've offered and provided things for others, and in doing so, I've

done good, I receive merits, and develop noble virtues by fulfilling responsibilities towards others and treating others the way one would like to be treated, and giving up killing, stealing, sexual misconduct, false speech, backbiting, abusive speech, meaningless speech, wrong means of livelihood and wrong view by reflecting; "If someone were to steal from me, I wouldn't like that, and similarly, if I will steal, someone else will not like that, so I will not steal; If someone were to engage in meaningless conversation, I wouldn't like that, and similarly, if I will engage in meaningless conversation, someone else will not like that, so I will not engage in meaningless conversation, and carry out good conduct in this manner in daily life.

Wrong vision refers to not understanding that merits can be gained by giving, making offerings to others, and not understanding the law of Karma. The Training Path that leads to Nibbana contains different levels of progress, different levels of attainments; two different levels can be seen across the ordinary state and noble states. Yet another levels of progress can be seen across four noble states.

A person who has an ordinary state of a mind can be said to have the right view, if the person has a reasonable understanding and acceptance of Karma and Buddha's teachings, which indicate that there is no permanent self, and, in doing so, living a righteous life. When comparing an ordinary mind state to a stream entry mind state understanding the teachings and the confidence in Buddha and his teachings are stronger at the stream entry stage. This confidence grows progressively to become greater when reaching the Arahantship. Similarly, other faculties (Energy, Mindfulness, Concentration, and Wisdom) tend to grow more and more at each stage of Nibbana, as one progresses in the training path leading to the four stages of Nibbana.

Chapter Five

NIBBANA: THOUGHTS & SELF-VIEW

The world is created in one's thoughts. When too many thoughts occupy one's mind, one may experience tiredness and weariness. Removing attachment to thoughts across fourfold Nibbana can bring satisfaction.

To gain to Stream Entry, what needs to develop in one's mind is that not get attached to one's thoughts that are creating self-view, and the view of society (eg. rituals) and others. Getting attached to one's thought process creates the self-view and "I". From "I" comes experiencing delight and non-delight, gains and losses, happiness and unhappiness, sufferings, and samsara. Not getting attached to one's thoughts across four stages bring, an end to one's samsara.

Following standards that are established within societies, and ordinary ways, the vast majority of individuals in the world have a tendency in their minds to get attached to their thoughts. By following standards, one goes with the flow; ordinary ways of doing things creates samsara. To go beyond standards requires training to not get attached to one's thoughts, which means to be free of greed, hate and delusion based on thoughts that create a view of "self", others, and society. For example, when someone gets attached to their thoughts that make up "I" or their self-view, they may experience pride; because of pride, they may experience restlessness, as they always want to receive priority for themselves. When someone experiences delusion, they may divide the universally applicable teachings based on social divisions; they may think that they are better than others or that they may divide their life experiences as good or bad, and teachings in many ways.

One way of understanding one's level of attainment of Nibbana or whether they are still ordinary is to analyse their thoughts, which are often expressed in their speech or writing. For example, those who identify Dhamma practice as living in the present moment in their speech or writing (indicating a tendency to grasp such a moment or thought), those who identify Buddha's teachings as a religion, a tradition, a division, a life style, a meditation practice, such as living in the present moment, those who give too much value to rules, and various identities (Western Buddhism etc.) are yet to develop the understanding required to gain fourfold Nibbana that is universally applicable to all.

The benefits of Buddha's teachings are to experience them immediately while living daily life, and Dhamma leads to Nibbana, which teaches how to live a satisfied life within one's lifestyle. Therefore, Nibbana can be experienced by anyone anywhere within their lifestyle, including a university students, politicians, artists and so on. Anyone can experience Nibbana if they train their minds in the right manner while doing other things in their lives as they wish and irrespective of external factors.

By reducing getting attached to one's thoughts that cause sufferings in the mind and thoughts that bind oneself to society and rituals, one gets to experience more satisfaction day and night while still possessing the desire for sensual experiences, and that's what the mind state of a steam winner is. Ordinary people possess the desire for sensual pleasures, they may identify their experiences as belonging to them, both happiness and unhappiness in mind as events take place. On the contrary, as events happen, Stream Winners get to experience satisfaction due to having lessened the degree of getting attached to their thoughts and relevant fetters.

All bad things that happen in the world are not happening to the self. Knowing that generates satisfaction in the mind of a Stream Winner as opposed to an ordinary person who grasps both good and bad due to self-view, happiness and unhappiness based on self-view created in one's thoughts. In this manner, as one progresses, one becomes free of getting attached to thoughts that are binding to fetters across fourfold Nibbana. A

Sotapanna still remains bound to amusement and enjoyment, and, knowing that there is no permanent self, they remain satisfied in their thoughts and make the most of their lives by doing what is beneficial to them and others. One example is a doctor, who may be a happy person, a genuine doctor who cares for others. Another may be a politician, who genuinely cares for others and so on.

Chapter Six

NIBBANA: TRAINING IN THOUGHTS & SAMSARA

Samsara is created in one's thoughts, from one thought through to another. The practice leading to Nibbana requires not getting attached to one's thoughts in daily life, because accepting that there is a self, a world, other things, and others are created in one's thoughts.

Theoretically, the commonly used word "delusion" means getting attached to one's thoughts. Thoughts are created autonomously without an owner. Thinking that thoughts are self is where the self and the world are created. So, a mind that is created based on a standard way of thinking and ordinary ways tends to accept "self" as "self" that is made up in one's thoughts, accept "society" as what is made up as "society" in one's thoughts, and live in a life that is made up as life and world in one's thoughts. Getting attached to made up things can generate stress and dissatisfaction.

Nibbana: Giving up getting attached to one's thoughts, that is renouncing based on noble ways.

Sometimes thoughts can bring happiness, sometimes unhappiness. Sometimes thoughts are generated based on what is happening in the external world. Sometimes thoughts happen on their own. Thoughts may wonder in a made-up past, a made-up present, or a made-up future, and so on. When someone tries to hold onto made-up things in thoughts, since made-up things are not the truth, they don't last, and they change. For example, when a "self" is made up, others and the world in thoughts, as they change, can bring distress and dissatisfaction in the mind.

Similarly, grasping a made-up self, society and the world, and things that are happening to form, including illness and similar things, can generate thoughts such as happiness, unhappiness, gains, losses, and similar things, and, if one will continue to grasp a made-up self, the world and society can bring a lot of distress and dissatisfaction specially when things are changing. Events happen that are beyond our control, such as birth, death, illnesses, losses and similar things, and clinging to things that are not controllable makes little sense. Things that are not under our control can bring suffering, and, by understanding how much harm one's thoughts can do to oneself, a wise person will reflect wisely and not grasp one's thoughts and self that are made in thoughts, society and similar things but simply be functional; do what is best for oneself and others without too much holding on to one's thoughts or grasping but be free of such things, a practice that requires being free of thoughts or Nibbana.

Before gaining Stream Entry, practitioners may give different values to different things, but, to train for higher wisdom, the practice requires training the mind to not grasp thoughts. Before gaining Stream Entry, a person may need to be in some kind of control and concentration to manage impurity in their thoughts, speech, and body. A person can give up the need for precepts and conscious concentration by developing the right understanding of deep Dhamma at Stream Entry, along with the right vision comes the right speech and bodily actions and the entire noble path has to be developed by developing one's vision.

Sakadagami state is somewhat similar to Stream Entry state due to the relevant fetters. After Stream Entry, it is worth concentrating on the impurity of the body and similar things to give up grasping thoughts related to sensual desires, and ill will, to becoming an Anagami.

For an Arahant, cessation or cease to exist in mind applies; eating is simply for eating, dressing is simply for dressing, speaking is merely for speaking, thoughts are mere thoughts, but being free of getting attached to one's thoughts will make up a practical person who is able to do beneficial things without grasping and, for example, for an arahant, living in a forest, and not living in a forest will be the same in their minds, as they are not grasping anything. Thus, Arahant is not a person who is living a life in one way, dressing in a particular way, speaking in a particular way, or living in a particular way; rather a person who is free of such particular ways, someone who is free of abiding to thoughts through cessation, has abandoned greed and hate, meaning not showing differential treatment for others or having pride or a desire to gain for oneself or clinging to one way or another but someone free of binding to fetters and simply doing whatever benefits others. An Arahant is functional without grasping meaning, they breath air, drink water, eat food, dress whatever and speak using common words without grasping such things or giving too much value to such things. Arahants are free of giving too much value and no giving value to such things, holding on to what they did yesterday, what they will do today or in the future, what they eat, where they live, what they hear, what they see, and similar things. They use words simply as words without grasping, which means that arahants are not proud and have no desire to gain materials for themselves. They show no differential treatment to others, they don't think they are superior, worse, or similar to others, or they don't divide teachings based on identities, but they respect Buddha, his teachings, and all other beings to the highest level.

So, the teachings that lead to Nibbana will be understood by those who are open minded and wise enough to see beyond standard ways. Thus, sila alone, meditation or concentration alone, or theoretical knowledge alone, rituals alone, are not sufficient unless one develops the understanding to see beyond ordinary ways to gain Nibbana. For example, while sila can be taken by many as rules, the matter of seeing beyond can be subject to one's wisdom and may be understood only by the wise. Thus, Nibbana can be gained in mind by thinking wisely to understand beyond ordinary ways.

Chapter Seven

THE PRACTICE LEADING TO STREAM ENTRY

The noble eightfold path leading to enlightenment begins with the right view. Right view through direct knowledge comes to establish when one attains Sothapanna and when that happens, at once, three fetters are eliminated (self-view, doubts about Buddha, Dhamma and noble Sangha, and attachments for rites and rituals).

Birth in Nobel linage happens at a random instance just like birth for beings out of socially created rites and rituals. Thus, Nibbana is not about a lifestyle that is created and accepted by social standards but a happening at a universal level like birth for beings.

There is a training path and practice that leads to the four stages of enlightenment and having a full comprehension of enlightenment means clearly understanding and reaching the four stages of enlightenment and the practice leading to each stage of enlightenment.

Each state of Nibbana differs and the practice requires for developing each stage differs. To train the mind in a way leading to Nibbana, developing four factors of stream-entry, and abandoning the fetters are relevant.

Teachings are about understanding. To gain stream entry, by understanding that there is no permanent self, one can try to develop a mindset that is not shaken due to the ups and down of life, which should be practiced in daily life.

By understanding that karmic events are relevant and not rites and rituals, one can practice the teachings in a way that leads to Nibbana genuine to one's heart, paying homage to qualities of Buddha and his teachings, and noble disciples in thoughts as much as possible within a day and in a way that will lead to ending samsara and suffering.

By clarifying doubts to understand the teachings, one can see the true message of Buddha leading to Nibbana. Given that Nibbana involves karmic influence, it is important to develop the four factors of stream-entry to gain Nibbana. The three factors include developing confirmed confidence in Buddha, his teachings, and noble Sangha. In practice, this can be done by attending to Triple Gem, and reflecting the qualities of the Triple Gem. Similarly, reflecting on the qualities of the Triple Gem generates joy, and joy leads to better concentration. One thing leads to another, and these factors are linked.

Buddha processes infinite good qualities, the highest degree of all humans and gods. Thereafter, an arahant, a disciple of Buddha, possesses lesser wisdom and inner qualities comparable to a supreme Buddha, and Sotappana will possess less wisdom in comparison to a Sakadagami and so on. By depending on Triple Gem and seeking refuge, one will soon end suffering for oneself. It can be said that, knowingly or unknowingly, all practitioners across the world take refuge in the same Triple Gem despite socially created divisions, books, and similar things.

The practice that leads to Nibbana or refuge always begins with Buddha, Sangha who sees Buddha, and Buddha's Dhamma, which means that those who understand Buddha and his teaching leading to four-fold Nibbana are the direct disciples of Buddha, noble Sangha. Noble Sangha, the third element of the Triple Gem, is not a replacement for supreme Buddha, because giving value to another teacher more than one would value supreme Buddha will prevent Nibbana for those who practice such a way.

Triple Gem follows an order for reasons. Giving value and respect to the Triple Gem (and respecting one's family, parents, friends, and those who deserve respect) is beneficial for all practitioners while they are in an ordinary mind state, before stream entry and across the stages of Nibbana to abandon both value and non-value (respect and non-respect) through cessation at Arahantship. Arahants of Buddha's training ways respect all beings without discriminating. Similarly, noble Sangha follows an order for reasons. Arahant is the highest stage of the Sangha order, and Sotapanna is the preliminary of the noble Sangha order. The order that we see in the Triple Gem and noble Sangha is not the kind of order we see in common ways, order established through years in practice, etc.

In societies, we see that, when there is an order, those who are in higher positions of the hierarchy tend to possess more gains and respect, while those who are in lower ranks tend to be treated differently. Yet, in the noble path of Buddha's way, those who are in the highest order are the ones who will provide the most wisdom, good inner qualities, and benefit to others, such that they will be able to provide teachings leading to Nibbana, merits, greater care, and respect for others.

Sangha becomes noble to the extent that they develop wisdom and inner qualities such as humility, gentleness, non-discrimination, and other qualities that are similar to Buddha across four-fold Nibbana. Sangha becomes Sangha to the extent that they refuge in noble Sangha.

Much needed friendship for gaining Nibbana, noble Sangha becomes a refuge for other friends when they are enlightened across four-fold Nibbana themselves, and they can explain the way of training the mind to lead to Nibbana and provide merits for shaping karma.

Fourth factor of Stream Entry refers to developing noble virtues; noble virtues can be developed by treating others in the manner one would like to be treated, maintain noble precepts (abstain from killing living beings, stealing, sexual misconduct, false speech, backbiting, harsh or abusive speech, useless or meaningless conversation, wrong means of livelihood), becoming a good person who looks after others as applicable to oneself (it may be looking after friends, family, an employer or employees, ascetics and so forth), and becoming an ethical person who genuinely cares for others and avoids discriminating against others on any grounds is the practice that is helpful in developing noble virtues, a factor of stream entry.

The path that leads to Nibbana is based on universally applicable karma, and everyone who has fulfilled the requirement of merits for gaining Stream Entry, influenced by their karma, can gain a state of Stream Entry at a random instance. In other words, when they get to hear teachings leading to Nibbana, they will want to listen, and their own karma will make it possible for them to make sense of teachings beyond ordinary views when they get to hear such teachings from noble ones. Otherwise, even if the message is readily available, they will be unable to recognize and make sense of the teachings, and, eventually, their own karma will shape their ability to gain Nibbana.

In sum, the practice leading to Nibbana should include multiple aspects that reflect the qualities of the Triple Gem in thoughts as much as possible in daily life and abandoning fetters through middle mind training. This requires within daily life maintaining the mind in the middle way; becoming a good person in all areas of life; and not discriminating against self or others based on social divisions. It also requires engaging in meritorious activities, maintaining precepts in daily life and engaging in Dhamma activities to facilitate the process of leading to Stream-entry and beyond.

Chapter Eight

CONFIDENCE IN TRIPLE GEM & STREAM ENTRY

Perfect confidence in Buddha, his teachings, and noble Sangha comes from gaining the realization of non-self-view at the first stage of enlightenment (i.e Sotapanna). The realization that there is no unchanging permanent self also leads to non-attachment to any rites and rituals. It is depending on Buddha, his teachings and Nobel Sangha that one can seek refuge and attain to Nibbana or gain merits. Those who attain stream entry will possess perfect confidence in Buddha, Dhamma, and noble Sangha, and noble virtues or morals. Therefore, those who want to attain stream-entry will benefit by developing these qualities. In terms of training, it will be beneficial to combine the practice of reflecting on non-self-view along with reflecting the qualities of Buddha, Dhamma, and noble Sangha as a reflection or a form of meditation to begin with and to integrate such reflections more into daily life with the purpose of developing confirmed confidence in the Triple Gem.

The entire training path leading to Nibbana depend on noble friendship, and it has been customary that noble friends will share the teachings of Buddha leading to Nibbana beyond what is commonly known among friends; immeasurable loving kindness and genuine care towards all friends without an ego and without desires, as all friends are a community who belong together.

In other words, meeting with the Triple Gem is the entry point to stream-entry. Meeting with the Triple Gem means gaining a deepened understanding of Buddha and his teachings and noble disciples of Buddha who carry the message of Buddha or the teachings of the Buddha leading to Nibbana. A noble disciple will live with Buddha and his teachings day and night. This is to say that the training in the disciple route requires one to train to abandon fetters by depending on Buddha and his teachings. In terms of training, this means reflecting on Buddha's qualities (" Supreme Buddha, the Gracious One, the Enlightened One, the Worthy One, the Perfect Sambuddha, the one who possesses all understanding to the highest level, and noble conduct to the highest standard, the Fortunate One, the one who understands the world, the unsurpassed guide for those people who need instructing, the Teacher of gods and humans, the Supreme Buddha, the Gracious One") and his teachings ("The Dhamma has been well-taught by the Gracious One, it is visible for those who practice Dhamma in the correct manner, Dhamma will produce immediately fruition for those who practice in the correct manner, others can be invited for inspection and seeing for themselves, Dhamma lead onward to Nibbana and the progress can be expected for those who practice Dhamma in the correct manner, Dhamma can be understood by the wise who can see beyond ordinary ways")

Given that Nibbana is a natural process that happens due to merits, and the teachings are universally applicable and go beyond social practices, social ordination is not relevant to gaining Nibbana. This is to say that whatever lifestyle allows one to develop the right understanding is what is beneficial for them, as it will allow them to abandon suffering. Both those who have and those who have not ordained based on social practices can become noble disciples of Buddha.

In other words, social ordination and ordination in the noble lineage differ; ordination in the noble lineage indicates meeting with Buddha and his teachings directly in one's heart and gaining a deeper understanding of the teachings. This can be achieved by cleansing the mind through proper techniques. Ordination in the noble linage is open to anyone who is practicing the teachings genuine to one's heart to meet the noble standards irrespective of external factors, divisions or rites and rituals. Noble friends are meant to be friends for life, and all friends are meant to care and support each other and all.

Why develop conformed confidence in Triple Gem?

Merits, Nibbana and Triple Gem are linked. Merits can be gained in many ways, such as becoming a good person who looks after friends and family members, which generate merits. Becoming a good person indicates training to develop noble virtues, one aspect of the four factors of stream-entry. It is the highest degree of merits that supports the highest blessings in one's life, which is Nibbana. The highest degree of merits can be generated by honoring, paying homage to, and attending to Budda, Private Buddhas, Arahants, Non-returners, Once-returners, and Stream entrees in order. These merits help to gain good things in this life, the afterlife, and Nibbana.

Purity, as an inner quality support, shapes Karma. Purity, as an inner quality and mental detachment, can be developed by practicing the teachings of Buddha in honesty to one's heart. Practicing the teachings in line with honesty in the heart produces noble Sangha, which is why a stream enterer abandons clinging to rites and rituals and precepts. Thus, reflecting on the qualities of the Triple Gem as a meditation can support developing four factors of steam entry, and, similarly, associating with those who have abandoned greed, hate, and delusion or being a noble friend who supports others gain merits and Nibbana, and good things in this life and afterlife. Refuge in Triple Gem shapes karma and provides merits that support the wellbeing of beings.

Family and ordinary friends can provide support while a person is living, and their help can be greatly appreciated. However, they are not able to help gain complete security in Samsara, and complete release from suffering in one's mind. Therefore, a wise person would think beyond ordinary ways for the benefit of self and accumulate merits for the benefit of this life and afterlife, by paying reverence to the Triple Gem and abandoning fetters to gain Nibbana should they wish to, and end samsara.

Below is a guided reflection that can be used in daily life to seek refuge in the Triple Gem:

To the Buddha I go for refuge.

To the Dhamma I go for refuge.

To the noble Saṅgha I go for refuge.

For the second time, to the Buddha I go for refuge. For the second time, to the Dhamma I go for refuge. For the second time, to the noble Saṅgha I go for refuge.

For the third time, to the Buddha I go for refuge. For the third time, to the Dhamma I go for refuge. For the third time, to the noble Saṅgha I go for refuge.

The Buddha, the gracious one, the worthy one, the perfect Sammasambuddha.

The Buddha endowed with supreme knowledge, and immense compassion.

The Buddha is endowed with highest degree of noble virtues and highest purity in conduct.

The Buddha, the blessed one, the one who understand the worlds.

The Buddha understood Dhamma by himself and showed us the correct way to train the mind to cessation, Nibbana.

The Buddha is completely free of greed, hate and delusion.

Buddha is the unsurpassed guide for those people who need guidance and instructing.

The Buddha, the Teacher of gods and humans.

Buddha possesses supreme knowledge, and compassion for all beings, Buddha awakens good people as the sun does the lotus.

I revere the Supreme Buddha as the highest refuge.

I am paying homage to the Buddha and shall follow his teaching to end suffering, and live life with satisfaction.

Chapter Nine

BEYOND ORDINARY VIEWS

One of the ordinary ways of describing Nibbana as a concept can be that sometimes it is described as happiness, a fearless state of mind. Yet, Nibbana is the end of births or samsara, functioning at a universal level just like a birth for beings shaped by one's merits and karma. All practitioners across the world, practicing in various ways or following divisions, if they want to gain four-fold Nibbana, require middle mind training, developing confirmed confidence in the Triple Gem and abandoning the fetters. Therefore, ignoring aspects of karma and merits that are shaping the birth of beings and some of the ordinary practices, such as maintaining momentary mindfulness as a meditation practice alone if applied as a practice leading to Nibbana, is insufficient for gaining Nibbana, because the practice leading to Nibbana is based on developing merits based on Triple Gem and shaping one's karma.

Ordinary ways of identifying Dhamma may include religion, division, rites and rituals, ceremonies, or lifestyle based on social practices. Before reaching a state of stream-entry, subject to individual differences, one may possess identities and may give too much value to such views. Abandoning clinging to such identities requires progressive training in the mind across training.

Two of the commonly spoken topics are virtues and meditation. Meditation as a conscious effort to reflect is needed only until one becomes a stream enterer. Similarly, virtues as precepts or monastic training rules are a preliminary practice that is required before the stream entry stage. After the stream entry stage, clinging to virtues is abandoned, because they are no longer needed, and the need to maintain the virtues through conscious efforts is given up when one possesses the right understandings of the teachings at the same time, abandoning the relevant fetters and gaining confidence in the Triple Gem. This happens, because, when there is deeper understanding that there is no permanent self, such an understanding naturally abandons greed, hate and delusion in one's mind, and the same understanding establishes noble virtues. By understanding the deep teachings and practicing in line with such teachings in daily life, one will become a Stream Winner. The noble path leading to Nibbana can be achieved by gaining a deeper understanding of the universally applicable teachings and by practicing in line with the teachings within one's lifestyle.

To go beyond commonly practiced virtues to gain stream entry, practicing noble precepts, treating others as the way one would like to be treated, becoming a good person who looks after others as applicable to oneself (it may be looking after friends, family, an employer or employees), and becoming an ethical person who genuinely cares for others and avoids discriminating against others on any grounds is the practice that is helpful in developing noble virtues, a factor of stream entry. Given that Nibbana is shaped by one's Karma and merits, it is one's genuine practice of abandoning greed, hate and delusion and developing mental detachment that contribute towards progressing in the practice leading to Nibbana, and noble virtues generate merits and allows one to shape one's Karma. The other three factors of stream entry are confirmed confidence in the Triple Gem, which can be developed by reflecting the qualities of Triple Gem in thoughts as often as possible within daily life. Paying homage and attending to the Triple Gem allow one to gather the highest merits required to gain Nibbana and good things in life.

Another commonly spoken topics is renunciation. According to ordinary thinking patterns and social standards that are created based on ordinary thinking patterns, renunciation may indicate giving up homelife or material things. Noble thinking patterns and standards go beyond ordinary thinking patterns, and renunciation indicates giving up mental attachment. For example, giving up things physically is alone unlikely to produce mental detachment. In that case, we can expect those who have given up physical things in life (food, accommodation, etc.) or rather those individuals who have been forced to give up necessities due to circumstances beyond their control should become naturally awakened when they are faced with experiencing lack of materials or requisites. But, without requisites, survival is not possible, and without surviving, the training leading to Nibbana is not possible, and all disciples of the Buddha are encouraged to get the requisites and the material things that are needed for survival and training in a middle way. Since the "middle way" is subject to an individual, the training leading to Nibbana is comfortable, as it does not require training in extreme ways. Giving up mentally is the kind of renunciation, that indicates giving up getting attached to one's thoughts (both desire to experience things and desire not to experience things and so on) that leads to Nibbana, and mental renunciation can be achieved by following the teachings in the way leading to Nibbana within one's lifestyle by training one's mind to gain cessation (Nibbana).

The common way to divide people as men and women, a householder and a monk is not applicable to Nibbana, since the universally applicable law of karma are applicable to all beings beyond divisions that are created by societies. The training path may appear restrictive before Stream Entry, as restrictions can help control a mind that lacks purity due to self-view made up in one's thoughts. Thus, before Stream Entry, one may take precents to develop noble virtues, engage in meditation to develop confirmed confidence in Triple Gem, and become a better person fulfilling responsibilities towards others. One may reflect on non-self-view by hearing regular Dhamma talks from Arahants and practicing middle mind training in daily life. In this manner, one will be able to gain the benefits of a practice.

One of the common views is that Nibbana indicates living in the present moment. For example, some of the common meditation practices such as death meditation, loving kindness meditation, living in the present moment and similar meditation practices alone is not sufficient for gaining Nibbana, Nibbana is not a meditation practice. Nibbana is a process that happens naturally shaped by karma and merits. Put differently, it is something in the air that enlightens a person shaped by merits and karmic effects. Consequently, rites and rituals that are created at the societal level do not impact the universal functioning that determines natural phenomena such as birth, death, and the enlightenment of beings. Enlightenment becomes a natural phenomenon due to the completion of paramis in the previous birth and is shaped by merits and karma for beings. The practice that leads to Nibbana is different from the practice that does not lead to Nibbana. For example, absence of Triple Gem in practice, such as living in the present movement through conscious effort as a mediative practice (or loving kindness meditation practice, death meditation practice), will not likely produce fruition, because living in the present moment as a stand-alone practice does not support the accumulation of merits across the four stages of Nibbana, and each stage differs. Thus, as discussed earlier in this book, in terms of practice, training to develop four factors of Stream Entry includes training to develop noble virtues and the other three factors. Meeting with the Triple Gem will allow other friends to hear the teachings beyond what is commonly known. While Triple Gem remains unchanged despite traditions, noble friends who share others pain and happiness without a gain and desires are meant to be genuine friends for life, a starting point of a noble path that begins with genuine friendship. Sangha is meant to support and look after one another without discriminating, a community of friends who genuinely care for one another and all.

Similarly, it may be that based on ordinary standards, an elderly person means an older person due to age. In line with noble standards, an elder means someone who has abandoned greed, hate, and delusion.

Based on convention, bhikkhu indicates someone who lives a monk lifestyle based on rituals, yet based on noble standards, bhikkhu means Sotappanna to Arahant, someone who has given up self-view and the relevant fetters.

The Conventional Sangha (Bhikku and householders: monastic and non-monastic Sangha) can practice Dhamma rightly or wrongly. Conventional Sangha is not the bhikkhu in noble path. Noble path lies beyond ordinary ways.

The monastic and non-monastic Sangha who practice Dhamma in the correct way may become an "Ariya-puggala" or a noble person to be included in the Sangha of Triple Gem.

The noble ones (Ariya Sangha) are practicing Dhamma in the correct way. One who attains the first stage of enlightenment (Sotapanna) will no longer be born in the animal womb, in hell realms, or as a hungry ghost. Below we shall explore what Nibbana is and address a few related questions.

What is ordination?

Ordination based on ordinary ways refers to living a lifestyle of a monk based on rituals.

Ordination based on noble ways refers to gaining Sotapanna to Arahantship.

What is Dhamma?

Dhamma meaning Sotapanna to Arahantship.

What is Sasana and Vinaya?

Sasana and Vinaya is Sotapanna to Arahant.

What is Nibbana?

Nibbana is Sotapanna to Arahant, the four stages of enlightenment, and the practices that lead to each of these stages of Nibbana differ. Those who practice the teachings in the right way in a manner that leads to Stream-entry will be able to attain Nibbana. Stream-entry or entering the stream is about gaining a deep understanding of the teachings of the Buddha and are open to anyone regardless of external factors, for example whether one prefers to live in a house, a forest, or a monastery, and his teachings allow individuals to practice Dhamma based on their personal choices and lifestyles.

Nibbana is not about a lifestyle.

Nibbana is not about traditions, divisions, or Buddhist schools.

Nibbana is not a philosophy or set of words or textbooks.

Nibbana is not living in the present moment or a meditation practice.

Nibbana is fruition that is established in one's mind due to the right practice of Dhamma. Therefore, the most important aspect of the teachings is to know how to practice them in a way that will lead to Nibbana.

How can one move from an ordinary understanding of the teachings to gain the understanding of a stream-enterer and beyond? Let us explore some examples below:

Why is Nibbana a not a lifestyle?

Nibbana is not a lifestyle. This is because Nibbana is to be experienced in one's mind, and it cannot be experienced in a lifestyle, as a lifestyle itself is created in one's mind. To train to cessation or Nibbana meaning train to give up getting attached to one's thoughts that make up the presence of self-view, lifestyle, view of others, materials, and the world in one's mind. Nibbana requires middle mind training and not a lifestyle training. Training in mind, and middle way training can be developed within any lifestyle.

Similarly, lifestyle indicates living a life in a particular way, and one person's lifestyle may not be suitable or feasible for another person. If Nibbana was a lifestyle, given that a person is different from another, there are individual differences, individuals have different circumstances, not being able to follow a lifestyle would have prevented a person's opportunity to gain Nibbana. Yet, Dhamma (meaning Nibbana; Sotapanna to Arahathship) is perfect in the beginning, perfect in the middle, and perfect in the end, so that anyone can train their mind to gain cessation while living a lifestyle that is suitable and feasible for them. Nibbana is about training the mind to becoming free of getting delight and non-delight in a lifestyle and similar things.

Middle-way training is a subjective process, one person's middle-way training in mind may not be applicable to another. Middle-way training in the mind can be developed to abandon getting attached to one's thoughts related to desire (i.e. "desire to experience things" and "desire to not experience things"). For example, a king who follows middle-way training in mind might consume certain food items that may seem like luxury food items to another. Yet, in his mind, the king may have given up the "desire to experience" and the "desire not to experience" taste.

Why Nibbana is not a tradition, division, and Buddhist schools?

It appears that one of the common views is that thinking Buddha's teachings are about traditions, divisions, and Buddhist schools. However, tradition, divisions, and Buddhist schools are created at the societal level, but Nibbana is functioning at the Universal level, and Nibbana is shaped by one's merits and karma. Therefore, how societies divide the teaching based on ordinary views is not what Nibbana is, as Nibbana is a universal happening, a birth in noble lineage.

What about textbooks?

To a greater extent, only the theory can be found in textbooks, considering whether or not the authors of the books heave gained Nibbana, one may want to choose wisely and understand Nibbana.

What about rites and rituals?

Teachings of the Buddha are universally applicable, therefore, socially created rites and rituals, ceremonies and divisions are not relevant to gaining Nibbana.

Rituals (dress code, language used, books etc.) may differ across societies, yet the practice remains universally applicable. Given that the teachings leading to Nibbana are based on the right understanding, anyone anywhere practicing correctly can gain Nibbana.

Similarly, performing rituals alone does not indicate one can develop in the path leading to Nibbana. For example, a person who is unable to develop wisdom (i.e right vision/right understanding) and maintain basic ethics (noble ethics), and who treats others badly can still perform a ritual but he or she will not progress in the path leading to Nibbana without developing the wisdom, and inner qualities.

Practice leading to Nibbana includes multiple components. In terms of practice leading to stream entry, abandoning fetters is relevant. The first three fetters can be abandoned through the right understanding.

Understanding that there is no permanent self, one can train the mind not to get too upset by bad events and not to get too happy due to good events or the middle way, and, in doing so, train the mind to remain unattached mentally in daily life. Factors of stream-entry can be developed by reflecting the qualities of the Triple Gem.

Why is the practice leading to Nibbana is the same for all despite divided ordinary views and divided social practices.?

Nibbana is a happening like birth for beings, and Nibbana is shaped by universally applicable karma. Thus, the practice leading to Nibbana remains the same for all, and Triple Gem remains the same for all.

There is a unified training path to all, which is universally applicable to entering into Stream Entry and which is based on developing the right view and gaining a deep understanding. Before reaching a state of Stream-entry, subject to individual differences, one may possess identities and may give too much value to such views. Abandoning clinging to such identities requires progressive training in the mind.

Divisions are created for not understanding Nibbana. By understanding and applying such an understanding to one's practice, one can abandon clinging to identities including divisions.

At the beginning of one's practice, before reaching a mind state of a Stream-enterer, **one may take precepts or monastic rules, gain a theoretical knowledge of Dhamma, listen**

to Dhamma from Arahants, associate with noble people, develop concentration, live in a suitable location, engage in education and business activities, engage in wholesome activities and create merits by attending to Triple Gem, become a good person; respect others, maintain loving kindness towards others, look after friends and family and others, discuss Dhamma on due occasions and apply Dhamma in daily life, avoid unwholesome activities, and thereafter gradually develop a higher understanding of Dhamma across four stages.

Is living in the present moment a Nibbana?

It appears that one of the common or ordinary views is that the technique to gain realization is living in the present moment and being aware. Yet, living in the present moment can occur with an underlying tendency to cling and for the majority of ordinary people, it would be possible for them to be aware in the present moment with fetters. Thus, living in the present moment and being aware is not the technique to gain Nibbana.

To gain realization, there is a need to go beyond commonly used techniques to developing four factors of stream-entry and abandoning fetters by being aware in the present moment, it is likely one can meet Triple Gem that is the entry point of stream-entry to abandoning non-self-view, doubts and clinging to rites and rituals.

The practice leading to Nibbana differs from the practices that do not lead to Nibbana. Momentary awareness is maintained through conscious efforts, which is how the ordinary understanding of Dhamma can be interrupted and may be unlikely to be stable. This explains why, for an ordinary person, there is continued existence (samsara). However, if maintaining momentary awareness as a meditation practice can be supported by the Triple Gem to generate merits (giving, reflecting, or mediating the qualities of the Triple Gem, and developing noble virtues indicates looking after others as applicable to oneself and avoiding discriminating against others on many grounds), in a way leading to developing four factors of stream-entry and abandoning fetters (develop middle mind training in daily life within one's lifestyle to abandon self-view and abandon clinging to divisions, ceremonies, rites, and rituals), such a noble practice will lead to gaining blissful Nibbana.

To understand sublime Dhamma leading to Nibbana and to be able to apply the teachings to one's life, one's wisdom helps, because, to gain the mind of a Stream-enterer, one needs to go beyond ordinary views and practices. To practice the noble eightfold path in the correct way, that just means understanding the

Dhamma beyond ordinary ways, one must gain the right understanding of what Buddha taught by gaining at least the first stage of enlightenment.

Given that Nibbana is happening at the mental level, external factors are not a contributory factor but developing highest understanding, wisdom, and good inner qualities. Buddha's teaching provides a uniform path leading to enlightenment and all Arahants understand and show the same path. Although it appears that the practice leading to Nibbana is interpreted in many ways across societies and the reason why many views exist regarding Dhamma practice including divisions is simply due to understanding of Dhamma among ordinary people can differ. Although understanding of Dhamma can differ among ordinary people, the deep understanding of Dhamma (Dhamma itself meaning Sotapanna and above) among noble people does not differ (except for their level of attainment) but remains the same, and those who have gained understanding up to Arahanship for themselves, they can explain the training to others with reasons. Without gaining a deep understanding of for oneself, it is unreasonable to expect one can explain the training path (or the Dhamma leading to Nibbana) to another as it would be a saying without knowing and explain the training path without knowing will be an irresponsible act on behalf of someone explaining the training path to Nibbana as such an act can mislead and prevent Nibbana for others or those who seek for it. This is why it was normal to declare attainment of enlightenment during Buddha's time so that they can explain the practice to others, and those who have truly attained to such a state declare such attainment without bringing themselves in to the picture, without an ego or desire for gains for themselves but simply for others gain. Wrong training path can prevent others for gaining Nibbana as for centuries, it is rare to find noble ones, and those who have gained to right understanding, declaring their knowledge without bringing themselves into picture, ego and desires and sharing their understanding with others in a humble manner without desires for gaining for themselves in a humble manner , and without any discrimination and desires is a noble act, it has been an ancient practice, and the path leading to Nibbana depend on noble friends. Noble friends will share the teachings of Buddha leading to Nibbana beyond what is commonly known among friends; immeasurable loving kindness and genuine care towards all friends without an ego and without desires, as all friends are a community who belong together.

One who gains the right understanding or view at the first stage of enlightenment (or who attains the stream entry) is capable in practicing the noble eightfold path in the correct way. Thus, one who attain the first stage of enlightenment is guaranteed to become an Arahant. For those who wish to attain enlightenment, it will be beneficial to put extra efforts in attaining the first stage of enlightenment.

Chapter Ten

MIDDLE WAY

The practice of Dhamma leading to Nibbana can be developed by understanding and applying the understanding to oneself in a middle way. Although there are several components of the practice, middle way mind training is a major component of the training of mind leading to cessation (Nibbana).

How can one train mental detachment in a middle way?

Although Nibbana across four stages is a progressive process, each stage when it happens, it happens fast. The state of stream entry (Sotapanna) happen in a moment of time, and Sotapanna might last a few moments. But, because a Sotapanna is unable to sustain such thoughts day and night, Sotapanna remains bonded to sense desires and higher fetters. Thus, practice leading to Nibbana is not a conscious maintenance of a thought process. Rather, the practice is about developing merits (developing four factors of stream entry), and abandoning fetters (self-view, rites and rituals, doubts) through middle mind training. A birth in the noble lineage is a natural process, the most important step in one's samsara.

A key aspect of the practice of Dhamma leading to Nibbana can be developed by understanding and applying the understanding to oneself in a middle way.

A tendency of an untrained mind is that it tends to cling to two sides, such as the desire to experience (or liking to experience things) and the desire not to experience (or dislike towards experiencing things), and when the mind functions in these two sides, it can produce stress when things are changing by nature and when they change, they can bring sufferings, and because changing things bring suffering knowing that can help one to maintain stable mind under any circumstance and not clinging in a way to Anagami state, and give up middle mind training later.

Similarly, one can abandon fetters (non-self-view, rites and rituals, precepts, doubts) by practicing in the middle way, may it be a text book, division, or the lifestyle of a monk, or lifestyle of a householder, saying "I have a lifestyle" or " I do not have a lifestyle" indicates two sides and the middle way training meaning, having or not having should be given equal value or importance, in doing so simply use what is available for improving wisdom and deep understanding of Dhamma, higher wisdom towards Arahantship and become a good person without clinging to such things. Clinging is not a helpful practice when such clinging give rise to identity views (for example, divisions that are socially created) and strengthens such views.

For example, someone who has self-view, they may experience pride when they gain materials, knowledge and similar things, and they may use whatever they possess may it be monetary gains, knowledge, skills and similar things solely for the benefit of self and this contradicts the Dhamma practice leading to Nibbana. An aspect of the practice of Dhamma leading to Nibbana requires sharing with others as Buddha did in a humble and gentle manner without desire for gains, a noble act. Similarly, becoming proud of possessing various skills, knowing the content given in books, or following a lifestyle and similar qualities that one needs to abandon in the practice leading to Nibbana to develop inner qualities. Thus, in practice, when a person who has gained to higher wisdom or Arahantship they would declare their attainment with good intention, without bringing themselves into picture, in a humble and gentle manner simply so other friends can hear the practice leading to Nibbana should they wish to, and they may end sufferings for themselves in practicing the teachings leading to Nibbana.

CHAPTER ELEVEN

GRASPING & CLINGING

Practice in a middle way meaning reduce clinging to things to reach cessation (Arahantship), and how can one reduce clinging to things in a practical manner?

The practice requires training the mind to understand beyond ordinary ways "against the current ways of thinking and doing". For example, ordinary ways of thinking, such as "I am happy" (I have a desire to experience) or "I am not happy" (I don't have a desire to experience) when things change, can generate stress. Instead, reverse thinking or thinking beyond ordinary ways in a middle way requires, giving up getting attached to one's thoughts that function in dual ways. For example, clinging to the lifestyle of a monk (desire for gains, honor) is equivalent to clinging to the lifestyle of a house-holder (desire for gains, honor, etc), clinging can be reduced by reducing the value given to things in mind by understanding impermanent nature of such things, may it be the lifestyle of a monk, or lifestyle of a householder, saying "I have a lifestyle" or " I do not have a lifestyle" indicates two sides and the middle way training meaning, having or not having should be given equal value or importance, in doing so not clinging to such things.

Let's take another example, happiness is one side and unhappiness is another side, middle way practice meaning not clinging to "happiness" or "unhappiness" by understanding both happiness and unhappy states are impermanent and what is impermanent, and when they change, they can bring sufferings, and because changing things bring suffering knowing that can help one to maintain stable mind under any circumstance and not clinging in a way to Anagami state, and give up middle mind training later.

Similarly, clinging to other things can be reduced by simply using things for the purpose without giving too much value to such things in mind by understanding the impermanent nature of such things, may it be the lifestyle of a monk or the lifestyle of a householder. Saying "I have a lifestyle" or "I do not have a lifestyle" (or I follow a tradition or I do not follow a tradition) indicates two sides, and the middle way training, meaning having or not having, should be given equal value or importance, in doing so not clinging to such things. The practice leading to Nibbana is progressive, and each stage of Nibbana differs and the practice required for each stage differs.

Chapter Twelve

FETTERS

Nibbana includes four stages, and it begins with the stream entry stage. Across four stages of Nibbana, to reach cessation at Arahant stage, there are ten fetters that need abandoning, giving up grasping in one's mind:

> Self-identity views, doubts about Buddha and his teachings, grasping at rites, rituals, precepts
>
> Sensual desire, & ill will
>
> Passion for form, passion for what is formless, conceit, restlessness, & ignorance.

Given that the fetters abandoned at each stage differ, certain practices are more beneficial for attaining the stream entry than the other practices.

A Sotapanna is free of getting attached to thoughts that make up self-view, rituals, and doubts. An Anagami is free of getting attached to thoughts that make up self-view, rituals, and doubts, sensual desires, and ill will. An Arahant is free of getting attached to thoughts that make up self-view, rituals, and doubts, sensual desires, and ill will, Passion for form, passion for what is formless, conceit, restlessness, & ignorance.

First thing first, the right view is gained at the stream entry stage and leads to progressing along the path leading to Nibbana. The noble eightfold path begins here. True knowledge begins with abandoning the relevant fetters; clinging to self-views, clinging to rites and rituals, and abandoning doubts along with coming to possess the four factors of stream-entry. Regarding the practice of abandoning the relevant fetters, one can train to abandon a non-self view by training the mind in the middle way in daily life.

How can one abandon clinging or giving too much value to self-view?

Developing middle mind training is helpful in abandoning self-view in daily life. By understanding that there is no permeant self, one can train the mind in the middle way to minimise stress. By understanding that life is impermanent and that ups and downs are part of life for all of us and are universally applicable to all beings, one can train the mind not to become disheartened when faced with bad events and, similarly, not to become overjoyed when experiencing good events, as they do not last long, and, in doing so, train the mind in the middle way in daily life (middle mind training is given up at the arahant state to lead to cessation; until then, middle mind training is useful). When supported by other factors, such as abandoning the relevant fetters by understanding that they are based on the teachings and by developing the factors of stream entry and supportive factors such as merits and precepts, one can practice the teachings in a way that will lead to Nibbana.

How can one abandon relevant fetters to gain Stream Entry?

Fetters can be given by middle mind training. Regarding doubts, to become a noble person or an enlightened disciple of Buddha, rites and rituals, ceremonies, schools and traditions, external factors (gender, age, appearance, nationality etc.) are not relevant, but one's level of gaining a deeper understanding of the stages of Nibbana (or attainment of Nibbana) and the extent of abandoning greed, hate and delusion is what applies. Given that Nibbana happens naturally shaped by Karma and merits, anyone anywhere practicing the teachings in a right manner will be able to gain fruition.

Based on ordinary ways of seeing things, typically, along with self-view, other views or identities (e.g., schools, divisions, or traditions) may come to exist in one's mind. Yet, the practice leading to Nibbana is the opposite to what is commonly practiced within societies, which is that not identifying schools and divisions is the right practice leading to Nibbana. This means simply to use whatever sources are available without clinging to them or identifying them to develop factors of steam entry. For a stream-enterer who has no-self view, there exist no other identities, and clinging to social identities, schools, and divisions cease to exist in such a mind state. While societies encourage self-views, social divisions, rites, and rituals, the teaching of Buddha leading to Nibbana opposes standard social practices. In terms of practice, this means that, for practitioners who are seeking Nibbana, there is a need to think and apply such reflections in practice to daily life to see beyond ordinary social practices. For example, society seems to suggest that people must go to the forest to attain Nibbana. Yet, if we were to think about it, one who lives in the forest and gets attached to the forest is unlikely to attain Nibbana, but those who live with Dhamma (meaning non-attached to self and things in any environment) will attain Nibbana. Right practice means practicing the teachings genuine to one's heart without clinging to identities in practice.

Apart from abandoning fetters, developing four factors of stream entry is an important practice. Developing four factors of steam entry means developing merits by attending to Triple Gem and becoming a good person. Merits can be developed by reflecting and paying homage to the Triple Gem in one's thoughts, developing generosity and maintaining ethics and loving kindness in one's heart. Maintaining ethics means something beyond precepts and rules in line with noble ways; ethics means avoid clinging to social divisions but becoming a good person who genuinely cares for others without any discrimination.

Given that Nibbana is shaped by Karma, one can practice genuine to one's heart and, in doing so, develop merits that support Nibbana and many good things in life and after life. Until one gains the right view in which Nibbana begins, one will face endless births, deaths, and samsara. Nibbana happens in its own time and is shaped by one's meritorious deeds and karmic influences. The teachings are open to anyone regardless of whether one prefers to live in a house, a forest, or a monastery, and his teachings allow individuals to practice Dhamma based on their personal choices and lifestyles.

Chapter Thirteen

VIPASSANA & NOBLE SEEING

To understand sublime Dhamma leading to Nibbana and to be able to apply the teachings to one's life, one's wisdom helps, because, to gain the mind of a stream-enterer, one needs to go beyond ordinary views and practices.

For example, vipassana means gaining a superior seeing or understanding or developing insight, and how it is understood based on ordinary view and practice differs from the noble way of practicing insight development. Based on ordinary understanding, the techniques to gain insight or super-seeing (vipassana) indicates living in the present moment and letting go. A noble understanding of insight development indicates developing the right view of a stream enterer, an entry point of gaining a deeper understanding of the Triple Gem to develop four factors of Stream-entry and abandoning three fetters by understanding the deep Dhamma taught by Buddha. The noble view of vipassana indicates Sotapanna, Sakadagami, Anagami and Arahant. In the end, the practice leading to Nibbana is one for all. It is not about textbooks or divisions; it is about gaining a deeper understanding to see the united teachings that are applicable to all. It is not about the external factors but the extent to which one has developed four factors of stream entry and abandoned three fetters in practice that is relevant to gaining a mind state of a stream enterer.

Chapter Fourteen

DHAMMA, NON-DHAMMA & DIFFERENT LEVELS OF PROGRESS

Right view, right understanding is Dhamma. Wrong view, wrong understanding is non-Dhamma. Dhamma meaning Arahanthsip. Right view begins with Stream Entry stage. By developing the right view across fourfold Nibbana, wrong view can be abandoned.

The Training Path that leads to Nibbana contains different levels of progress, different levels of attainments; two different levels can be seen across the ordinary state and noble states. Yet another levels of progress can be seen across four noble states and In other words, Dhamma meaning Arahantship, and those who have understood Arahantship are the noble disciples who can represent the Buddha and his teachings to accepted noble standards and in the correct manner.

Wrong view of an ordinary person is not understanding the law of Karma. Right view of an ordinary person is understanding universally applicable law of karma. Progress in the Dhamma path is determined by one's levels of understanding, attainment across fourfold Nibbana and not determined by the number of years in practice, external factors (eg. age, gender, life style etc.) nor by memorized passages from textbooks.

Right view of a Sotapanna is possessing confirmed confidence in the Triple Gem and not grasping in to three fetters (self-view, rituals, precepts). Right view of a Sakadagami is confirmed confidence in the Triple Gem and abandoning the first three fetters. Right view of an Anagami is possessing confirmed confidence in the Triple Gem and abandoning sense desires, ill will and previous three fetters. Right view of an Arahant is giving up desire and not having desires to form (and other fetters); giving up middle and cessation. Thus, understanding of deep Dhamma differs based on one's level of attainment. Ideally, one should have completed four-fold Nibbana before explaining to another.

Lacking a full understanding of what Nibbana is, some practitioners mix up various other subjects and spend their time talking about things that are not directly relevant to gaining Nibbana. They may engage in doing things that are not part of a practice that leads to Nibbana. Due to their lack of training in the mind, they may possess a strong sense of self-view, and their minds will have a tendency to cling to various divisions, and their tendency of a mind of grasping to self-view can be expressed in their speech. They may divide the teachings based on division and geographical locations, because they are still ordinary and are yet to understand Dhamma practice, which is universally applicable to gaining Nibbana.

Not understanding Nibbana in full, ordinary views of Dhamma are many. Altered versions of teaching that are built upon incorrect views and that claim to be Buddha's teachings lead to confused Dhamma (non-Dhamma). The wrong understanding of Dhamma prevents Nibbana or liberation for those who aspire for it, and those who practice Dhamma in common ways. Right understanding of Dhamma will allow one to gain benefit of a practice.

Those who practice the teachings by understanding the teachings beyond ordinary understanding to reach the understanding of a stream-enterer will be able to gain realization. Right view of an ordinary person (mundate view) is acceptance of karma. Thus, all those who practice Dhamma, if they will be humble and honest to take the responsibility to self-declare their attainment before sharing Dhamma with others, this will be helpful for themselves and others to clarify Dhamma as Taught by Buddha. For example, ordinary friends can still discuss theoretical aspects of Dhamma by acknowledging that they are yet to gain a noble state and share Dhamma at the ordinary level. They can still gain benefits, such as materials that are needed for their survival, and, by continuing in their own practice, in that manner, Dhamma can be purified for the benefit of all.

The training path leading to Nibbana can be developed by developing one's understanding to gain an understanding of a Stream Winner.

By understanding what Dhamma and non-Dhamma are, understanding who is Buddha and non-Buddha's ways, understanding noble Sangha, and understanding Triple Gem, one can abandon fetters, and, by abandoning fetters, one can understand Triple Gem. Triple Gem and fetters are linked, and Dhamma means Triple Gem and Triple Gem means Dhamma. By eradicating doubts and gaining a clear comprehension, those who wish to aspire to Nibbana may fulfil their wishes.

Chapter Fifteen

USEFUL REFLECTIONS

Nibbana or awakening means four stages starting from Stream Entry.

The noble path leading to Nibbana can be achieved by gaining a deeper understanding of the universally applicable teachings and by practicing in line with the teachings within one's lifestyle.

Ordinary ways of practicing the teachings of Dhamma and noble ways differ. Subject to individual differences, ordinary ways of Dhamma practice may indicate clinging to rites and rituals, ceremonies, precepts or demand respect, materials and recognition, whereas noble ways indicate abandoning getting attached to one's thoughts, abandoning fetters, abandoning any thoughts that sharpens self-view such as pride, hate, wanting to gain and make use of materials simply for the benefit of self, and similar things, maintain thoughts about Triple Gem day and night, and becoming a good person who is fulfilling responsibilities to others, giving respect to others and not demanding in nature.

Below are some of the relevant questions:

How to develop Dhamma vision of a Stream Winner?

Continue living life and going and doing usual things, while hearing Dhamma from an Arahant, one can develop Dhamma vision of a Stream Winner. Applying Dhamma in to real life and by reflecting life experience from a Dhamma perspective, a person can expect to progress in the training path leading to Nibbana.

Practicing Dhamma to gain Nibbana requires training the mind to think beyond the ordinary within daily life. For example, when someone experiences a low mood, it is useful to bring back mindfulness and make some effort to reflect on the teachings of the Buddha that remind us how ups and downs are part of life, as that is the nature of life for all of us. Similarly, when one feels upset or worried, it is useful to bring back mindfulness to reflect that context can be anything, so that feelings and thoughts, good times and bad times are normal things to expect in life, and everything is subject to change universally applicable to all beings. Applying such a Dhamma perspective into analyzing real-life experience is a helpful practice to maintain peace of mind.

Similarly, becoming an ethical person at the stream entry level requires abandoning discriminating self and beings, something beyond practicing precepts and training rules, and becoming a responsible person who genuinely cares for self and others in all areas of life to become a good friend, a good parent, a good sibling, and likewise by developing good internal qualities and ethics. Similarly, practicing to reach Nibbana (stream-entry and beyond) requires more than meditation, because what happens during meditation is usually one attempt to withhold temporarily the autonomous functioning of the mind (thoughts, feelings) by focusing on a meditation object or a particular aspect. Therefore, typically, meditation can provide short-term relief or effect. Gaining Nibbana requires identifying the mind's autonomous functioning as nonself. To get there, it is useful to move beyond temporary meditation practice to apply the Dhamma perspective into daily life. This explains why it is useful to train the mind in the "middle-way" in daily life, as this practice allows not withholding autonomous functioning but reducing getting attached to the autonomous functioning of the mind or reducing identifying the mind as "self".

Furthermore, for those who aspire to attain enlightenment, as a form of training, it will be beneficial to combine the practice of reflect on non-self-view in daily life and the qualities of Buddha, Dhamma, and noble Sangha to eliminate the first three fetters and to gain the non-self-view.

Below is a guided reflection that can be applied to giving up getting attached to one's thoughts related to self-view in daily life:

1. "I am subject to decay, all beings are subject to decay, I have not gone beyond decay,"

2. "I am subject to illnesses, and all beings are subject to illnesses, and I have not gone beyond illnesses,"

3. "I am subject to death, and all beings are subject to death, and I have not gone beyond death,"

4. "I am the owner of my karma, all beings are subject to their karma, and I am not gone beyond my karma,"

5. "All that is mine, dear and delightful are subject to change," is always to be reflected upon.

6. "All that I wish, and I want, I will not get as the way I wish, and I like!" is always to be reflected upon.

Regarding the practice of abandoning the relevant fetters, one can train to abandon a non-self-view by training the mind in the middle way in daily life. Practice in a middle way means reducing clinging to things to reach cessation (Arahantship).

How can one reduce clinging to things in a practical manner? For example, clinging to the lifestyle of a monk (desire for gains, honour) is equivalent to clinging to the lifestyle of a householder (desire for gains, honour, etc.). Clinging can be reduced by reducing the value given to things in mind by understanding the impermanent nature of such things, may it be the lifestyle of a monk or the lifestyle of a householder. Saying "I have a lifestyle" or "I do not have a lifestyle" ("I have a religion"; "I do not have a religion"; "I am happy" and "I am not happy") indicates two sides, and the middle way training, meaning having or not having, should be given equal value or importance in one's mind, in doing so not clinging to such things. Similarly, clinging to "expectations" and not having expectations" indicates two sides, and the middle way training, meaning having or not having, should be given equal value or importance, in doing so not clinging to such things. By understanding that both having expectations and not having expectations in thoughts are subject to change, when they change, they can bring suffering. Because changing things can bring suffering, knowing that can help one to maintain a stable mind under any circumstances, to not cling in a way to the Anagami state, and to give up middle mind training later.

In this manner, by understanding that life is impermanent and that ups and downs are part of life for all of us and are universally applicable to all beings, one can train the mind not to become disheartened when faced with bad events and, similarly, not to become overjoyed when experiencing good events, as they do not last long, and, in doing so, train the mind in the middle way in daily life (middle mind training is given up at the arahant state to lead to cessation; until then, middle mind training is useful). Regarding doubts, to become a noble person or an enlightened disciple of Buddha, rites and rituals, ceremonies, schools and traditions, external factors (gender, age, appearance, nationality etc.) are not relevant, but one's level of gaining a deeper understanding of the stages of Nibbana (or attainment of Nibbana) and the extent of abandoning greed, hate and delusion is what applies.

Factors of Stream-entry can be developed by reflecting the qualities of the Triple Gem, and attending to the Triple Gem.

Given that Nibbana happens naturally shaped by Karma and merits, anyone anywhere practicing the teachings in a right manner will be able to gain fruition. Merits can be gained in many ways, such as becoming a good person who looks after friends and family members (as applicable to oneself), which generate merits. Becoming a good person indicates training to develop noble virtues, one aspect of the four factors of stream-entry. It is the highest degree of merits that supports the highest blessings in one's life, which is Nibbana. The highest degree of merits can be generated by reflecting the qualities of the Triple Gem, honoring, paying homage to the Triple Gem, and attending to Buddha, private Buddhas, arahants, non-returners, once-returners, and stream enterers in order. These merits help to gain good things in this life, the afterlife, and Nibbana.

The Triple Gem remains unchanged despite divisions or traditions, as the Triple Gem indicates Buddha, his teachings leading to Nibbana and his enlightened disciples irrespective of tradition or schools. Refuge in Triple Gem shapes karma and provides merits that support the well-being of beings. Sangha is a community of friends. Friends who follow the teachings may carry different levels of deep understanding of the teachings of Buddha depending on their level of attainment across four stages of enlightenment or whether they have reached a noble state or are ordinary and are still practicing becoming a noble person. Sangha meant to look after one another and all. In other words, meeting with the Triple Gem is the entry point to stream-entry. Meeting with the Triple Gem means gaining a deepened understanding of Buddha and his teachings and noble disciples of Buddha who carry the message of Buddha or the teachings of the Buddha leading to Nibbana.

Recollecting or reflecting on the qualities of the Buddha, Dhamma and noble Sangha and attending to Triple Gem in one's thoughts (speech and actions) is a useful way to get into Buddha's path, and that is how one can receive ordination in noble linage, accumulate merit, and to eliminate first three fetters to achieve enlightenment. By deepening one's understanding of Triple Gem, one can gain to Stream Entry. By gaining a deeper understanding of the teachings of Buddha, one can abandon doubts. Along with attending to Triple Gem, if one will develop middle-mind training to abandon fetters, that will help practitioners for gaining Stream Entry.

In sum, in terms of practice leading to Nibbana, to abandon non-self-view, understanding that there is no permanent self, one can train the mind not to get too much upset by bad events and not to get too much happy due to good events or the middle way, and, in doing so, train the mind to remain unattached mentally in daily life. Similarly, an aspect of the practice of Dhamma leading to Nibbana requires **developing inner qualities such as sharing with others,** in a humble and gentle manner without desire for gains for oneself, without pride, and engage in doing such noble acts in daily life, and fulfil responsibilities towards others, and not treat others differently due to many grounds, social divisions in daily life, and developing merits by reflecting the qualities of the Triple Gem, and attending to Triple Gem and Supreme Buddha, Arahant, Anagami, Sakadagami, Sotapanna, ordinary faith followers, Dhamma follower in order, and this is the kind of practice that will help practitioners to gain to Stream Entry state, as noble path requires developing wisdom and inner qualities that of similar to Buddhas. To gain Nibbana (noble Sangha route) that is universally applicable, the practice remains the same for all.

Guideline for Training Leading to Nibbana

Avoid doing bad things, doing wholesome things, and purifying one's own mind, these are the teachings of all Buddhas.
It is good to have the patience to reach the highest Arahantship, as it is a progressive path.
All Awakened Ones agree Nibbana is the highest blessing.
Those who cause others harm and discomfort are unable to find peace. Those who oppress others based on social divisions or any other ways are not yet peaceful.
Try and become a better person fulfilling responsibilities to others, and this will help to develop noble virtues.

By training the mind to the middle way, one can abandon stress. Nibbana happens on its own time, a natural process.

It is shaped by Karma, and it depends on its merits. Paying homage to the Triple Gem in thoughts generate merits and merits and Nibbana are linked.

By abandoning three fetters and developing four factors of Stream-entry, one can gain Stream Entry.

Becoming a good person who genuinely cares for others and becoming an ethical person who abandons clinging to identities and social divisions and avoids discriminating against self and others based on such divisions, something that requires more than practicing precepts and training rules. Understanding that Nibbana happens due to merits and is shaped by Kar-ma, try to practice the teachings genuine to the heart without clinging to rites, and rituals, such a practice is required to gain noble virtues.

Mindfully, try not to get attached to thoughts that create the past or think excessively about the thoughts that create the future, or create too many expectations of the future. Whatever quality is present is right here, but it too passes away. Therefore, find peace in the present moment.

Mindfully, try and not to get attached to thoughts that generate stress, pain, sufferings in many ways: anxiety, hopelessness, helplessness, and similar ways.

In life, there are things we cannot change, and this is applicable to all of us. It is pointless to worry over things that cannot change, instead make the most of this day, and make the most of life.

Training the mind in a middle way, not taking in, not giving too much value, or not clinging, that's how we develop the heart to experience day-to-day.

By training the mind to the middle way, one can abandon stress. Nibbana happens on its own time, a natural process.

It is shaped by Karma, and it depends on its merits. Paying homage to the Triple Gem in thoughts generate merits and merits and Nibbana are linked.

By abandoning three fetters and developing four factors of Stream-entry, one can gain Stream Entry.

Chapter Sixteen

FURTHER THOUGHTS

In this book, I have discussed how can one train one's mind in a way gain to Stream Entry, and cessation or Nibbana, what to practice and what not to practice for gaining benefit of one's Dhamma practice in a way leading to Stream Entry.

Below is the summary of these key issues.

First, Triple Gem indicates Buddha, his teachings leading to Nibbana and his enlightened disciples irrespective of tradition or schools.

The Triple Gem remains the same for all practitioners despite socially created divisions.

Second, Nibbana is achieved through four progressive stages (Sotapanna, Sakadagami, Anagami and Arahant). Nibbana is fruition that is established in one's mind due to the right practice of Dhamma. The Training Path that leads to Nibbana contains different levels of progress, different levels of attainments; two different levels can be seen across the ordinary state and noble states. Yet another levels of progress can be seen across four noble states. Depending on a person's level of knowledge and inner qualities across stages (ordinary to Arahantship), a person will abandon sufferings and Samsara.

Stream Entry is not a consciously produced state but a natural process that happens in a random instance just like birth for beings. That moment allows a being to be born in the noble lineage and brings stable change in a being so that a person who was before stream entry will not be the one after stream entry. A person who becomes a Stream Winner comes to possess good inner qualities in an instant.

Third, Nibbana is a training in mind. the world is created in one's mind, and self-view and others are created in one's mind and in one's thoughts. To train to cessation or Nibbana, giving up in mind refers to giving up getting attached to one's thoughts that make up the presence of materials, the world, self-view, and others in one's mind. In other words, whatever material things that are physically present and whatever the world is physically present should not interfere with one's mind.

Fourth, the path that leads to Nibbana is based on universally applicable karma, and everyone who has fulfilled the requirement of merits for gaining Stream Entry, influenced by their karma, can gain a state of Stream Entry at a random instance. Birth in Nobel linage happens at a random instance just like birth for beings out of socially created rites and rituals. Thus,

Nibbana is not about a lifestyle that is created and accepted by social standards but a happening at a universal level like birth for beings.

Fifth, to gain to Stream Entry, what needs to develop in one's mind is that not get attached to one's thoughts that are creating self-view, and the view of society (eg. rituals) and others. Getting attached to one's thought process creates the self-view and "I". From "I" comes experiencing delight and non-delight, gains and losses, happiness and unhappiness, sufferings, and samsara. Not getting attached to one's thoughts across four stages bring, an end to one's samsara.

Sixth, the noble eightfold path leading to enlightenment begins with the right view. Right view through direct knowledge comes to establish when one attains Sothapanna and when that happens, at once, three fetters are eliminated (self-view, doubts about Buddha, Dhamma and noble Sangha, and attachments for rites and rituals).

Seventh, right view is Dhamma, and wrong view is non-Dhamma. Dhamma means Arahantship. Right view across Nibbana includes Stream Entry to Arahantship. Right view of an ordinary person is understanding universally applicable law of karma to a reasonable standard. One who gains the right understanding or view at the first stage of enlightenment (or who attains the stream entry) is capable in practicing the noble eightfold path in the correct way. Thus, one who attain the first stage of enlightenment is guaranteed to become an Arahant. For those who wish to attain enlightenment, it will be beneficial to put extra efforts in attaining the first stage of enlightenment.

Eighth, although Nibbana across four stages is a progressive process, each stage when it happens, it happens fast. The state of stream entry (Sotapanna) happens in a moment of time, and Sotapanna might last a few moments. But, because a Sotapanna is unable to sustain such thoughts day and night, Sotapanna remains bonded to sense desires and higher fetters. Thus, practice leading to Nibbana is not a conscious maintenance of a thought process. Rather, the practice is about developing merits (developing four factors of stream entry), and abandoning fetters (self-view, rites and rituals, doubts) through middle mind training. A birth in the noble lineage is a natural process, the most important step in one's samsara.

Ninth, based on ordinary understanding, the techniques to gain insight or super-seeing (vipassana) indicates living in the present moment and letting go. A noble understanding of insight development indicates developing the right view of a stream enterer, an entry point of gaining a deeper understanding of the Triple Gem to develop four factors of Stream-entry and abandoning three fetters by understanding the deep Dhamma taught by Buddha. The noble view of vipassana indicates Sotapanna, Sakadagami, Anagami and Arahat.

Tenth, the Training Path that leads to Nibbana contains different levels of progress, different levels of attainments; two different levels can be seen across the ordinary state and noble states. Yet another levels of progress can be seen across four noble states. Dhamma meaning Arahantship, and those who have understood Arahantship are the noble disciples who can represent the Buddha and his teachings to accepted noble standards and in the correct manner.

Eleventh, regarding fetters, at Sotapanna stage, one eliminates three mental fetters which are self-view, doubt of Buddha, Dhamma and noble Sangha, and attachments to rites and rituals including wrong practices. At Anagami level, one eliminates sensual desire and ill will.

Twelfth, the Sotapanna or the stream-enterer stage meaning "one who enters the stream, with the stream being the noble eightfold path. The stream-enterer has the perfect understanding of the Buddha, his teachings and noble Sangha. Thus, to gain to Stream Entry stage, one need to understand Triple Gem.

In sum, practicing leading to Nibbana at the entry level (or stream-entry stage) requires within daily life maintaining the mind in the middle; becoming a good person in all areas of life; and not discriminating against self or others based on social divisions, reflecting the qualities of the Triple Gem in thoughts and engaging in wholesome activities as much as possible in daily life.

The Dhamma is well-expounded by the Buddha. It is excellent in the beginning, excellent in the middle, and excellent in the end. It has no contradictions but is absolutely pure.

The beneficial results of the Dhamma can be made visible to every individual if they will practice in the correct manner.

The Dhamma is not constrained by time. Its beneficial effects can be realised immediately for those who practice Dhamma in the correct way. Dhamma is effective in all times; in the past, in the present and in the future.

The Dhamma is open to all partitioners to come and see for themselves. It is not mysterious; it will be visible for those who develop right understanding very clearly.

The Dhamma does not lead practitioners into fascination, into delusion, but leads to Nibbana.

The teaching of the Buddha points to a universally applicable truth which can be understood by a wise person who can see beyond ordinary ways when properly explained.

May all beings be well, may all beings be free and happy.

www.ingramcontent.com/pod-product-compliance
Lightning Source LLC
LaVergne TN
LVHW041609070526
838199LV00052B/3053